Harlan Page Beach

Knights of the Labarum

being studies in the lives of Judson, Duff, Mackenzie and Mackay

Harlan Page Beach

Knights of the Labarum
being studies in the lives of Judson, Duff, Mackenzie and Mackay

ISBN/EAN: 9783337285685

Printed in Europe, USA, Canada, Australia, Japan

Cover: Foto ©Andreas Hilbeck / pixelio.de

More available books at **www.hansebooks.com**

KNIGHTS OF THE LABARUM

BEING STUDIES IN THE LIVES OF
JUDSON, DUFF, MACKENZIE AND MACKAY

By HARLAN P. BEACH

*Educational Secretary of the Student Volunteer Movement
for Foreign Missions; formerly Missionary in China*

CHICAGO
STUDENT VOLUNTEER MOVEMENT
FOR FOREIGN MISSIONS
1896

EXPLANATORY

THIS little book does not claim to be a collection of finished biographies. Like a volume on India, issued a year ago, "The Cross in the Land of the Trident," it is intended as an outline text-book for Mission Study Classes, whether conducted by the Student Volunteer Movement, or carried on by Young Peoples' Societies and women's missionary organizations. The condensation of material and the use of bold-faced type and italics are due to the desire to facilitate the acquisition of leading facts and to suggest topics and sub-topics for further reading. The enthusiastic approval of many among the thousands who have used the similarly prepared book above mentioned, has encouraged the author to again make use of this style of writing, faulty though it may be from a typographical and literary point of view.

The author hopes that in addition to a mastery of these outline facts, the user will read the fuller, and hence more living and interesting, volumes from which he has derived most of his information. Several readings have been suggested by chapter or page at the close of each chapter, and in classes some of these, at least, should be read and reported upon as valuable side-light material. Only thus can the greatest profit be derived from these studies.

Leaders of classes should possess a full biography of each of the lives outlined here, and the following are suggested as the best now in print: "The Life of Adoniram Judson," by his son, Edward Judson, 1883, A. D. F. Randolph & Co., New York; the two-volume-in-one edition, published by the American Tract Society of New York, of "The Life of Alexander Duff, D. D., LL. D.," by George Smith, LL. D., 1879; "John Kenneth Mackenzie, Medical Missionary to China," by Mrs Bryson, Fleming H. Revell Company, New York and Chicago; and, "A. M. Mackay, Pioneer Missionary of the Church Missionary Society to Uganda," by his Sister, 1890, A. C. Armstrong & Son, New York.

The principal reason why these four have been chosen from among the many mighty men on the mission field is that they represent four different lines of missionary effort, as well as four different countries. A broader view of missionary life is thus secured than would have been the case if representatives of one land or of one phase of work were studied. This will partly account for the omission of some missionaries equally famous, though additional reasons for choosing these rather than others have also been operative. Thus the latter part of Livingstone's life, like that of Dr Peter Parker's, was only indirectly missionary, and both had severed their connection with missionary organizations. Again, Bishop Patteson and Dr Paton are omitted, because both of them labored in a field which has comparatively little connectional interest for American students, while in the case of Dr Paton, an additional reason for neglecting so marvelous a life is the fact that it has not yet reached its completion.

September, 1896.

CONTENTS

		PAGE
I.	Judson's Life from 1788 to 1816	9
II.	The Judsons' Burman Work	22
III.	Duff's Early Life and Educational Work	36
IV.	Duff as a Promoter of Missions	49
V.	The Man Mackenzie, His Field and People	63
VI.	Mackenzie, the Medical Missionary	76
VII	Mackay's Early Life and His African Field	89
VIII.	Mackay's Parishioners and His Work	101

Labarum, the sacred military standard of the early Christian Roman Emperors, was first adopted by Constantine the Great after his miraculous vision in 312. . . . A Special guard of fifty soldiers was appointed to protect the sacred standard.—Encyclopaedia Brittanica.

* * *

I determined not to know anything among you, save Jesus Christ, and him crucified. . . . I have fought the good fight, I have finished the course, I have kept the faith ; henceforth there is laid for me the crown of righteousness.
—St. Paul.

* * *

Thy servants will pass over, every man that is armed for war, before the Lord to battle.—Numbers xxxii. 27.

KNIGHTS OF THE LABARUM

I

JUDSON'S LIFE FROM 1788 TO 1816

IN MEMORIAM. REV. ADONIRAM JUDSON. BORN AUG. 9, 1788. DIED APRIL 12, 1850. MALDEN, HIS BIRTHPLACE. THE OCEAN, HIS SEPULCHRE. CONVERTED BURMANS, AND THE BURMAN BIBLE, HIS MONUMENT. HIS RECORD IS ON HIGH.

The above inscription, found on a marble tablet in the Baptist church at Malden, Mass., constitutes one of the interesting relics of America's early missionary history. Another, found in this same Boston suburb, is a wooden, two-storied and dormered house embowered in trees, the birthplace of "The Apostle of Burma."

Parentage. The person thus commemorated was the eldest of four children. *The father*, true to his Hebrew name, Adoniram, "Lord of height," was more like a Hebrew patriarch or Roman censor than fathers of to-day. Erect, above the ordinary height, grave and taciturn, stately and awe-inspiring, he occupied the lofty position of Congregational minister in the old-time New England community. It was his to command in the parish, and especially in his home, where he ruled as absolute monarch. Not ambitious for himself, he inordinately desired to see his children achieve greatness. To this end he largely threw the son on his own resources, and constantly held before him the possibility of becoming great. Christianity was to the father a thing surely proven and demanding immediate obedience, and any attempt to question it was tantamount to rebellion. In general his life was marked by inflexible integrity and uniform consistency, and called forth from the young Adoniram the phrase, "honored parent," as well as inspired in him self-reliance and overweening ambition. Paternal influence doubtless accounts for the stately courtesy and the dignified literary style of Judson's later years.

His mother, Abigail Brown, seconded her husband in his ambitious schemes for the boy; yet of her Augustine's words are also true: "This name of my Saviour, Thy Son, had my tender heart, even with my mother's milk, devoutly drunk in, and deeply cherished; and whatsoever was without that name, though never so learned, polished, or true, took not entire hold of me."

Anecdotes of His Boyhood. A sort of forcing system, of which in later life Judson did not approve, made of the child of three a reader in the Bible, and when four, a preacher to children, his favorite hymn being, "Go preach my gospel, saith the Lord." He is a philosopher and astronomer at seven, as he lies on his back at midday endeavoring to learn, by means of a hole in his hat, through which he long gazes at the sun, whether or not it moves. The problem was solved, but the boy could not tell the process. Later his success as riddle guesser brings him a whole book full of them, an arithmetic.

Preparatory and Collegiate Education. The coming of this book, which his father's praise and the fact of its being difficult made delightful, began his educational career. Arithmetic establishes his reputation. Navigation follows at ten years, and soon thereafter his odd hat, and proficiency in the classics studied at the grammar school, won him the nickname, "Old Vergil dug up." For leisure hours, he indulges in a *mélange* consisting of Ben Jonson's plays, novels of Richardson and Fielding, and theological works.

His studies, which he enjoyed far more than play, suffered a prolonged and almost fatal interruption at the age of fourteen, and for the first time he calmly considered the meaning of life. During convalescence, castle-building made him a nineteenth century Alexander weeping for unconquered worlds. Better impulses allured him to a life of Christian usefulness, lived to the glory of God; but as that meant being a Christian, and as he was determined to become a great man, these thoughts he foolishly set aside.

Providence College—the present *Brown University*—received Adoniram at sixteen, he having entered as sophomore. President Messer has testified, in a letter to Judson's father, to "a uniform propriety of conduct, as well as an intense application to study," while a classmate had "no recollection of his ever failing, or even hesitating in recitation." Quite naturally, therefore, and in spite of six weeks of teaching during senior year, he graduated with the valedictory in 1807. Unfortunately these years brought him in contact with French infidelity which so permeated educational centers at that time. Yielding to the flood, and especially to the arguments of a witty and talented upperclassman, Judson became a professed deist and looked forward to the law as an open door to political preferment, or to the stage as a field for his dramatic gifts.

Teacher and Author. Two weeks after receiving his B. A., Judson opened the "Plymouth Independent Academy," his father being then pastor in that historic town. His application during this year must have been unremitting, as, in addition to his school duties, he published two textbooks, "The Elements of English Grammar," and "The Young Ladies' Arithmetic," which, though exhibiting the "ingenious literary enterprise and perseverance" of their author, were of no great pedagogical value.

Judson's Conversion. In August, 1808, less than a week after closing his academy, he mounted a horse and set out on a tour through the North "to see the world." Fulton's newly invented steamboat and the charming scenery of the Hudson greatly interested him, but *questionable scenes* soon followed. Arriving in New York, he joined a band of strolling players in order to prepare himself for dramatical writing. He said later of these experiences: "We lived a reckless, vagabond life, lodging where we could, and bilking the landlord when we found opportunity. . . . Before leaving America, . . . I made a second tour over the same ground, carefully making amends to all whom I had injured."

His Damascus came soon after leaving New York, when

he returned to Connecticut for his horse. A godly young minister, supplying his uncle's pulpit at Sheffield, greatly impressed him. This added force to his father's severity and his mother's grief, exhibited when he told them, before leaving home, of his deistical beliefs. The night after leaving Sheffield, his room in the inn adjoined that of a dying young man whose future prospects disturbed his sleep. He tried to banish "superstitious illusions" by the thought of what his deistical college friend would say if he were cognizant of such fears. The morning brought the news of the young man's death and the crushing intelligence that the dead man was no other than this same college idol. Thunder-struck, Judson gave up his tour and turned Plymouth-ward, his mind deeply impressed with the need of salvation, but with the scales still unremoved from his eyes. Professors Griffin and Stuart of *Andover Seminary* advised him to enter that institution. This he finally decided to do, "not as a professor of religion and candidate for the ministry, but as a person deeply in earnest on the subject, and desirous of arriving at the truth." Having become somewhat proficient in Hebrew, Judson was able to enter the middle class at Andover, and here it was that the light came; though it was only the clearest evidence of the truth of Christianity and an increasing need of the Saviour that caused the conquered infidel to say, "My Lord and my God." December 2, 1808, was the date of this momentous decision, but not until the following May did he unite with his father's church.

Andover "Divinity College" Life, 1808-1810. Judson's conversion ended forever his old life of doubt and political and literary ambition. His supreme desire now was to know how he could order his life so as to best please God. That this thought might be constantly before him, he inscribed on several constantly used articles, "*Is it pleasing to God?*" His letters at this period glow with earnest desires after holiness and with whole-souled consecration to Christ's service. Without raising the question, he felt that he must devote his life to the ministry in some form. When as a student he went out to preach, his sermons were "solemn, impassioned, logical and highly scriptural, without much of the hortatory, and with no far-fetched figure or studied ornament of phrase." These addresses were rarely written : for, "why should I spend my time in attempting the correctness and elegancies of English literature, who expect to spend my days in talking to savages in vulgar style? Why not cultivate extempore speaking altogether, when that will soon be my only mode of preaching for life?"

His interest in missions began in September of his senior year, when he read Buchanan's "Star in the East." Later he did not consider this sermon remarkable, but at the time it produced a powerful effect on his mind, prevented his studying for several days, inflamed his mind with romantic ideas and sent him through the students' rooms declaiming on missions. The overdrawn pictures in Syme's "Embassay to Ava," added fuel to the flames and ended in a highly wrought enthusiasm, which never died. It was some time after this—in February, 1810—that the decision was reached. During a solitary walk in the woods behind the seminary, the difficulties in the way seemed so great that after meditating and praying on the subject, he inclined to give it up, when the force of Christ's last command so overwhelmed him that he resolved "to obey it at all hazards, *for the sake of pleasing the Lord Jesus Christ.*" His "passion for missions" was so great that he became a man of one idea, and was soon the leading advocate of the cause at Andover.

The First American Volunteer Movement. Most of the men drawn around him were from Williams College, where in a grove and under the shadow of a haystack the missionary fire was kindled among American students. In 1808 they had signed a constitution whose first, second, fifth and sixth articles pledged them to train themselves for missionary service, to personally establish a mission or missions among the heathen, to admit none as members who were under obligations preventing their going on a mission, and to hold themselves ready to go when and where duty might call. Judson did not sign this constitution until 1811, but speedily allied himself with them in prayer and in an active missionary propaganda in other colleges and seminaries and in the churches where called to preach. Most of the members had in mind temporary service and a mission to American Indians, but Mills, and especially Nott and Judson, desired Asia's conversion and a lifelong service.

Judson and the A. B. C. F. M. The American Board, though the first foreign missionary organization in America, had its forerunners. The Massachusetts Missionary Society, formed in 1799, altered its constitution so that in 1804 it was free to take up work abroad. Doctors Griffin and Worcester had urged most eloquently the claims of the heathen, while several thousand dollars had been sent from America to Carey and others. A missionary magazine, a predecessor of the American Board's "Missionary Herald," was published in 1803. Notwithstanding these facts, Judson and his associates were the ones who were the occasion of forming America's first foreign missionary organization.

In pursuance of *their policy* to interest influential clergymen in missions, a number of professors and ministers met in Professor Stuart's house at Andover, June 25, 1810, to whom their desire to enter on the work was made known. Their fervent prayers and serious deliberations led the next day to the *formulation of a plan for a board* as Doctors Worcester and Spring rode in a chaise to Bradford. There the representatives of the Massachusetts, New Hampshire and Connecticut Congregational Associations were to meet. An appeal to the Association, written out by Judson and signed also by Messrs Nott, Mills and Newell, asked counsel concerning their missionary duty, the field to be occupied, and the organization under which they were to work. Judson and the others were there to advocate the scheme. On June 29, 1810, a report was adopted and the first board of commissioners elected, though not until September 5, was the board finally constituted. The four petitioners were encouraged to go abroad as soon as possible.

To France and England. Judson, in the desire to place himself and companions on missionary soil, had written in April to Dr Bogue, in charge of the London Missionary Society's institution at Gosport, inquiring about India and Tartary as mission fields and asking assistance in preparation therefor. The Board having been formed and feeling unable to proceed alone, requested Judson to go to England and confer with that society concerning a co-operative work, and to secure and transmit to the Board "ample and correct information relating to missionary fields, the requisite preparations for missionary service, the most eligible methods of executing missions and generally whatever may be conducive to the missionary interest."

His voyage in the "Packet," his capture by a French privateer, imprisonment at Bayonne, escape therefrom, several weeks residence in France, during which time he travelled in one of Napoleon's carriages, his examination of the dark side of French life, ending in a sermon at a masked ball, constitute one of the exciting pages of his eventful history. Its value to him in later years he gratefully records.

Arriving *in England* he was very cordially received by the London Society, but his ardent wish to reach the field made him somewhat recreant to his duty. He not only did not make the investigations upon which he was to report to the Board, but finding that concert between the two societies was impracticable, he secured an appointment to India for himself, Nott, Newell and Hall, who took Mill's place in the list. At the meeting following his return, the Board were practically forced to commission and support the four candidates; otherwise they might have gone out under the London Society. Judson's pertinacity on this occasion received a mild censure which years afterward gave rise to a heated and profitless controversy, regretted in his calmer moments.

Counter Currents. Mr Judson met with other obstacles also. In 1809 he had received appointment as tutor in Providence College and later was asked to become a colleague of Dr Griffin in Park Street Church, the largest in Boston. In spite of his father's disappointment and the tears of mother and sister, he refused these flattering positions and set his face resolutely duty-ward. An apparently more serious obstacle was his delicate constitution with a tendency to consumption. His rigid adherence to *three rules of health*,—frequent inhalations of large quantities of air, daily sponging of the entire body in cold water, and systematic and vigorous walking,—enabled him to meet the health requirements of the Board and to reach a goodly age.

Embarkation and Voyage. When before the General Association at Bradford, Judson had been waited on by a fascinating Bradford Academy graduate, and ten days later an acquaintance began which ended in marriage on Feb. 5, 1812. The following day he and Messrs Nott, Newell, Hall and Rice were ordained in Salem, whence he sailed on the 19th for Calcutta, commissioned "to labor in Asia, either in the Burman Empire, or in Surat, or in Prince of Wales Island, or elsewhere." On board the brig "Caravan" were Newell and his illustrious wife, Harriet; the others sailed from Philadelphia on the ship "Harmony."

The appearance of Judson, then in his twenty-fourth year, is thus described: "He was at this time small and exceedingly delicate in figure, with a round, rosy face, which gave him the appearance of extreme youthfulness. His hair and eyes were of a dark shade of brown. . . His voice, however, was far from what would be expected of such a person and usually took the listener by surprise," so much so that a London minister, hearing him read a hymn, said of it: "If his faith is proportioned to his voice, he will drive the devil from all India."

During the voyage much time was devoted to *the study of baptism*. This was taken up as a preparation for the time when converts from heathenism with their families would be in his care, and also because he wrongly supposed that the Serampore Baptists, with whom he was to live for a time, would attack his pedobaptist views. Careful study, which in the case of many equally critical missionary students has led to different conclusions, caused him to accept the Baptist views. Hence, soon after his arrival in India, he and his wife were immersed, and Judson resigned his connection with the American Board, its missionaries and churches, —a heroic step which caused him deepest pain. Mr Rice was the only one of their company who shared his views, and he soon after returned to America to agitate and effect by voice, as Judson did by pen, the *formation of what is now the American Baptist Missionary Union*, one of our strongest boards. This step marked the beginning of the marvellous growth of that denomination.

Rejected of Men. Compelled by conscience to leave the

American Board, he was not wholly acceptable to his Baptist friends. Dr Carey felt that the luxurious upbringing of Americans unfitted them for the privations of missionary life, and so looked askance at him. *The East India Company*, too, fearing that the arrival of so many recruits would embarrass them in certain questionable practices, decreed their return to England, though by a kind providence the Judsons were allowed to go to Mauritius. Thence, two months later, they returned to Madras. They had planned to start a mission on Prince of Wales Island, but to avoid deportation to England, they were obliged to flee, and the only vessel available was bound for Rangoon. This crazy craft they regretfully boarded, as they regarded a mission to that city with great horror.

Arrival at Rangoon. The voyage was dangerous, but the Judsons finally reached Burma July 13, 1813. Their feelings after going ashore were among the most gloomy and distressing that they had ever known. The *house first occupied* was outside of the city walls near the execution ground, the cemetery and the dumping ground, and was exposed to robbers and wild beasts. Rangoon itself was then a poorly built, dirty, undrained city of 10,000 inhabitants, and was intersected by muddy creeks. Later, they lived within the walls, not far from Burma's most famous temple, the Golden Dagon Dagoba, glorying in eight of Buddha's hairs.

They were *not the first Burman workers*. In 1807 the English Baptists sent two men thither and later two others, one being William Carey's son Felix. The London mission sent two men in 1808, but their work ceased within a year. Mr Chater, a Baptist, had prepared a Burmese St Matthew, and Felix Carey accomplished something as linguist, vaccinator and printer. He was the only one there in 1813, and his subsequent wild career hindered missionary work in the Empire.

The Burman Field. Burma, now an Indian province, was then an independent and absolute despotism in spite of its many councilors and kingly advisers. Its "Lord of Life and Death," "Owner of the Sword," ruled a territory over 1000 miles long and 600 in breadth. The Nile-like plain of the Irawadi,—a future key of Asia,—the forest covered hills and mountains were then largely undeveloped, and intercommunication was difficult save by water. Its valuable timber lands were beast-infested and contained in some districts still fiercer men. Its inhabitants, incorrectly supposed by Judson to equal our own population at that time, were the prey of their governors, the "Eaters" of provinces. Law was always on the side of the largest bribe, while torture and diabolical punishment awaited the poor litigant.

The religion which Burma's apostle had to meet was Buddhism of the southern type, unrelieved by the theistic and soteriological hopes of China and Japan. Monasteries were on every street, and priests were reckoned as one out of thirty of the population. The doctrines most commonly remembered were connected with merit, which affected their transmigrations and their cheerless doctrine of Nirvana. In spite of this atheistic atmosphere, Yule could thus *describe the Burmans:* "They are cheerful and singularly alive to the ridiculous: buoyant, elastic, soon recovering from personal or domestic disaster. With little feeling of patriotism they are still attached to their homes, greatly so to their families; . . . Though ignorant, they are, when no mental exertion is required, inquisitive, and to a certain extent eager for information; . . . temperate, abstemious and hardy, but idle, with neither fixedness of purpose nor perseverance." Such a people might have been reasonably easy to reach, as there was no hereditary priesthood, caste, nor isolation of women; but the opposition of rulers and the death penalty which threatened those who turned from Buddhism, were tremendous obstacles. A comparatively rich literature, a religious terminology and compulsory primary education for boys were an aid to the missionary; but on the other hand, Burma had not a few stubborn disputants who, in their extravagant tenure of Idealism and Nihilism, would put Berkeley and Hume to shame.

Plan of Campaign. Though young Carey was absent, the Judsons did not confront this Gibralter alone; for they knew intimately Him in whom they believed, and placed themselves in His hands as implicitly as did their Serampore brethren, who spent fifteen days in prayer over one of the early steps in connection with the Burma Mission.

Mrs Judson says that *at first they had but one plan*, that of learning the Burmese most thoroughly. Later, Judson gained such command of the classical Pali as to fully equip him for his work. This was a difficult task. No English speaking teacher, dictionary nor adequate grammar was at hand, so that they had to blaze their way. Bent over a book-covered table beside a venerable pundit whose head was wrapped in a handkerchief and his loins with a cloth, the two chattered, read and took notes all day long. Meanwhile Mrs Judson acquired the tongue more rapidly, if less scientifically, while superintending the work of the house. Carey had so impressed upon Judson the value of accuracy in speech, that he delayed longer than wise, perhaps, before conducting public worship and doing zayat preaching. These duties did not begin until he had been in Burma nearly six years, though much personal work had been done from the beginning.

The language mastered, work must be planned in accordance with *Judson's deep-seated convictions*. Burman Buddhism taught that there was "no God to save, no soul to be saved, and no sin to be saved from." The opposite of these three doctrines he believed with his whole soul. He felt, moreover, that no Burman could reach heaven who did not realize his sin and flee to the Saviour. When they began their work not one of Burma's millions, so far as Judson knew, was a believer in Christ, nor even an earnest inquirer; and as they stood alone in that land, the crushing responsibility of their position deeply solemnized them. They believed, however, that here and there about them was a person so led by Providence and so influenced by the Spirit that if the story of salvation could reach him, he would accept it. To discover such persons was their task.

Their methods were simple. Judson did not believe that he was first a promoter of civilization, then an educator and finally a herald of salvation. The last function was pre-eminently his, and to accomplish his work he made large use of eye-gate and ear-gate. The Word of

God must, at the earliest possible moment, be accurately translated into the tongue of the people, and comprehensive and concrete statements of truth be sown in every promising field. Burman ears must also be filled with the saving message. Unlike many missionaries, Judson thought that the most strategic point of attack was the citadel of Mansoul instead of the weaker walls of Childsoul; hence, work for adults consumed most of his time.

The pair well knew that *a Christian atmosphere* was essential to the growth of the exotic with which they were entrusted. "God is love" must be taught through "I am love," and their lives in home and church, in zayat and in palace, must teach this, instead of relegating the duty to nicely framed mottoes. Tender sensibilities, strong affections, undying love were the saps through which they determined to zigzag toward Burman fortresses.

The Burman Mission in 1816. This, then, was the situation at the beginning of this year. Felix Carey had seceded from the mission, leaving the Judsons as the sole evangelizing force in a land containing several millions of Buddhists and heathen. Behind them were the Baptists of America, awakened to self-consciousness and missionary zeal largely through Judson. He in his twenty-eighth year and his wife a year younger, they had already gained tolerable mastery of the language, but no usable tract, grammar, dictionary, or portion of Scripture had yet been published, nor was there a single Protestant convert to preach through Burman lips evangelical Christianity. But God was there and in them; and their hopes, founded on His sure promises, flooded the eastern horizon with prophetic glory.

SUGGESTED READINGS.

Conant: The Earnest Man, (1856), Chs. I-XII.
Dowling: The Judson Offering, (1847), Pp. 1-44.
Eddy: The Three Mrs Judsons and Other Daughters of the Cross, (1860), Pp. 43-73.
Encyclopædia of Missions, (1891), Articles Adoniram and Ann Hasseltine Judson and Burma.
Hervey: The Story of Baptist Missions, (1884), Chs. XII, XIII.

Johnston: Life of Adoniram Judson, (1887), Chs. I-VII.
Mrs A. H. Judson: Mission to Burmah, (1823).
Edward Judson: Notable Baptists: Adoniram Judson, (1894), Chs. I-IV.
Knowles: Ann Hasseltine Judson, (1835), Chs. I-VII.
Page: Noble Workers, (1875), Pp. 201-209.
Pierson: New Acts of the Apostles, (1894), Pp. 105-110.
Piper and Maccracken: Lives of the Leaders of Our Church Universal, (1879), Pp. 837-842.
Pitman: Heroines of the Missionary Field, Pp. 278-293.
  Lady Missionaries to Foreign Lands, Pp. 13-64.
Richards: Adoniram Judson, (an Epic; 1889), Pp. 1-18.
Stuart: Lives of the Three Mrs Judsons, (1851), Pp. 13-180.
Thomson: Great Missionaries, (1862), Pp. 281-290.
Vanguard of the Christian Army, Pp. 77-89.
Walsh: Modern Heroes of the Mission Field, (1882), Pp. 63-75.
Wyeth: Missionary Memorials: Ann H. Judson, (1894).
Yonge: Pioneers and Founders, (1890), Pp. 117-128.
Edward Judson: The Life of Adoniram Judson, (1883). Early Years, Ch. I.; Consecration to Missionary Life, Ch. II.; Voyage to Burmah, Ch. III.; Burmah, Ch. IV.; Life in Rangoon, Ch. V.

II

THE JUDSONS' BURMAN WORK

His name alone is a tower of strength to the missionary cause; but his name is not alone. He was the center of a family group, to which, so far as I have read, no parallel can be found in ancient or in modern history. Ann, Sarah and Emily Judson—all three, noble, intellectual and Christian women, all three devoted and affectionate—sympathized with and shared in all his labors, rose to his height, and shine even beside him.—*Rev W. S. Mackay*, in the "Friend of India."

Story of the Years. A missionary experience, extending over nearly four decades, cannot be fully condensed into a few pages; yet Dr Judson has himself left a brief "Autobiographical Record of Dates and Events," which will aid us in fixing on the salient points of his career, with that of his devoted wives. Roughly outlined, their Burman life falls into six periods.

1. At Rangoon, 1813-1823. This period has already been partly described. In 1816 Judson, being kept from work by illness, prepared "Grammatical Notices of the Burman Language," and his first tract, "A View of the Christian Religion." In October they were reenforced by the Houghs. 1817 was marked by the completion of his translation of Matthew and the beginning of a Burman dictionary. 1818 was a sad year for them. Dr Judson had been broken down by four years of overwork on the language, in translating and in book-making; so he resolved to try *a sea voyage* to Chittagong, the southeast point of India proper, where were some Burmese-speaking converts of the Serampore Mission. He purposed to reorganize that scattered church and bring back helpers who could conduct worship in Burmese; but the expected short voyage was lengthened to about nine months, during which time Judson was driven to India and barely escaped death by fever and starvation. Mrs Judson suffered equally during his absence. All suppposed that her husband had been lost at sea. Government persecution assailed Mr Hough, who was rescued by her great tact and personal influence. Then cholera swept over the city and the Houghs proposed leaving. She was temporarily expecting to go with them, but at last decided that she would not desert the station while there was the least chance of her husband's return. Two new families came out in the fall.

In April of the following year *public worship and zayat preaching* began. This was followed in June, 1819, by the baptism of their *first convert*, Moung Nau, nearly six years after beginning work in Rangoon. A number of others including the philosopher, Shwa-gnong, becoming inquirers, the viceroy became alarmed and the work was stopped. Judson and Mr Colman resolved to go the Emperor in person and appeal for toleration, an eventful journey of two months resulting in nothing. Being unable to secure the lives of converts, Judson determined to transport them to Chittagong, where they would be under British protection. Their willingness to endure persecution and their request that he delay until a church of ten members was formed prevailed, and he remained, though the Colmans went thither to prepare a place of refuge. Mrs Judson's health being shattered, they were forced to go to Calcutta, where a three months' *rest at Serampore* was a refreshing oasis in their lives. Relief was only temporary, and a few months after their return home, Mrs Judson was obliged to sail for England and America, where she did much to create interest in the mission and to gain recruits.

During her absence he went, in 1822, with their newly arrived physician *to Ava*. His skill in removing cataracts had attracted the Emperor's notice, and an imperial summons brought them to the Golden Foot. Dr Price's ability secured to them an invitation to reside at the capital. After five months there, during which time Judson secured mission premises and pressed home the claims of Christ on princes, higher officials, and the Emperor himself, he returned to Rangoon. While awaiting for ten months the return of Mrs Judson, he completed on July 12, 1823, his translation of the New Testament, together with an epitome of the Old Testament, intended to serve as an introduction to the New.

2. *Prisoner at Ava and Oung-pen-la, 1824-1826.* The auspicious beginning of their life in Ava was early shrouded in gloom. The war cloud between England and Burma, due to the sheltering of Burman refugees in Chittagong, soon burst. As all white foreigners at the capital were regarded as spies, Dr Judson was seized on June 8, 1824, and an experience began equalled in suffering only by that of some early church and Catholic missionaries. *His official communication* on the subject is as follows: "Through the kind interposition of our Heavenly Father, our lives have been preserved in the most imminent danger, from the hand of the executioner, and in repeated instances of most alarming illness during my protracted imprisonment of one year and seven months—nine months in three pairs of fetters, two months in five, six months in one, and two months as prisoner at large. Subsequent to the latter period, I spent about six weeks in the house of the north governor of the palace, who petitioned for my release, and took me under his charge; and finally on the joyful 21st of February last [1826] I took leave with Mrs Judson and family, of the scenes of our sufferings." *No mention is here made* of the horror of those eleven months at Ava; of the march to Oung-pen-la, which was so severe that one of their number died on the road; no hint of the suspense due to their belief that they had been removed from the capital to be offered as a sacrifice to insure victory over the English; no suggestion of the filth, the heat, the hunger, the thirst, the lion cage, the deathly silence of the three o'clock hour, the nightly stringing on a bamboo pole, the "tender mercies" of the "Father" of the prison which was well named *Let-ma-yoon, i. e.,* Hand, shrink not; no such blood-curdling narratives as Mrs Judson's "The Kathayan Slave:" no; these details were left for others to record and any who choose may find them in Gouger's

"Narrative of Imprisonment in Burma." Enough for this sufferer that he was privileged to bear in his body the marks of the Lord Jesus.

3. At Amherst, 1826-1827. The war resulted, among other things, in the cession of the Tenasserim Provinces, and to escape Burman despotism the Judsons took the remaining four of their eighteen converts to Amherst, a new British settlement selected by the Commissioner and Dr Judson. Soon after arriving, he was asked to accompany the British envoy to Ava to negotiate a commercial treaty. This he only consented to do when assured that an effort would be made to insert a clause securing religious liberty to the Burmans. It was a trying experience. Ava was a hell full of awful memories; his days were filled with diplomatic wrestling which secured nothing in the way of religious toleration; and worst of all, during his absence his wife died of a fever from which his presence might have saved her. This terrible loss was followed just six months later by his little daughter's death, whom he left beside her mother underneath the hopia-tree and removed to Maulmain.

4. Maulmain, 1827-1845. Amherst proved to be less desirable than this new town, the headquarters of the British army, and so the mission was transferred thither. The years there were most useful ones. Beginning with *the ascetic period* of his life, they were brightened by red-letter days like those when Dr Judson baptized the one-hundreth Karen convert, and later—twenty-two years after landing in the country,—the one-hundreth Burman disciple. They witnessed in 1834 *his second marriage,* fruitful in work and bringing to his home eight children. They also saw the publication of some of his most valuable works, notably the New Testament and the quarto edition of *the Burman Bible,* and some of his best minor compositions. He did not remain all the time in Maulmain. Journeys to Rangoon, Prome, Tavoy, Calcutta, a second time with his family to Bengal, and later to the Isle of France, resulted in improved health and new impulses to work all along the line.

5. In the home land, 1845-1846. For thirty-three years

Judson had never seen a ship sailing out into the west without intensely longing to fly homeward; yet a stern regard for duty had kept him at his post. Finally, as his wife's life seemed at stake, he decided to return, though he took with him two Burman teachers, with whom he was to work each day on his dictionary. Reaching the Isle of France, Mrs Judson was so much better that the pair heroically determined to separate that he might return to his work, and he actually sent the teachers back, expecting soon to follow them. A relapse, however, caused him to follow his original plan. On reaching Napoleon's prison island, the gentle spirit departed and the body was laid away on St Helena's soil. As the bereaved hero approached Boston, he fell to worrying as to how to find a lodging place, little dreaming that thousands of homes longed for the privilege of receiving him, and that *the nine months of his stay in America* would be one continuous ovation, eagerly chronicled by the press, both secular and religious. Yet his presence brought some disappointment. A severe throat affection prevented prolonged public speech so that he was compelled to talk in a whisper to one who repeated it to the immense audiences. Moreover, his third of a century in Burma, had, as often happens with missionaries, unfitted him for the English of the platform, and an additional disappointment was his unwillingness to narrate his foreign adventures, especially the experiences of Oung-pen-la.

Nevertheless, these months brought the freshening of thought and religious life, so necessary to the missionary, enkindled in all denominations a new flame of missionary zeal, and more important to him, *acquainted him with Emily Chubbuck*, whom he married June 2, 1846. Within six weeks thereafter they turned their faces towards Burma, accompanied by five new recruits, and were wafted onward by a mighty volume of earnest prayer.

6. *Sunset years, 1846-1850.* On their arrival, the superior opportunities for finishing the dictionary, as also Judson's desire to be in the regions beyond, impelled them "to leave the twilight of Maulmain in order to penetrate the denser darkness of Rangoon," though "it seemed harder for him to leave Maulmain for Rangoon than to leave Bos-

ton for Maulmain." There, in a gloomy brick structure, which its many inhabitants caused them to call "Bat Castle," Judson worked like a galley-slave on his dictionary, while his wife applied herself to Burmese and to writing the story of her predecessor's life, characterized by Bishop Walsh as "one of the most exquisite biographies in the language." *Governmental intolerance* prevented any open religious work and made secret meetings extremely difficult. Then Bat Castle became a hospital, whose sick inmates could not secure nourishing food, being reduced on one occasion, though unwittingly, to a dinner of rats, which in their ignorance they declared excellent.

A desire to make at Ava one more appeal for religious toleration and the advantage to the dictionary from such a residence, were thwarted by the awful cry at home of *retrenchment* and even Rangoon had, for that reason, to be deserted. At Maulmain he completed the English-Burmese part of his dictionary and had brought the other part well on towards completion. Family joys, succeeded by his wife's serious illness, were followed by a lung affection of his own. Dysentery and congestive fever made a long sea-voyage necessary, and he bade his wife a last adieu on April 3rd. Some days of agony and then, after the farewell words, "It is done; I am going. . . . Take care of poor mistress," he fell asleep as quietly as a child, on April the 12th. At eight o'clock that evening the larboard port was opened and the body of him whose life had been bread cast on Burman waters was committed to his much loved ocean, three days distant from his adopted home.

The three Mrs Judsons. Before considering Judson's character and work, a glance should be taken at that noble trio, without whom his life would have lacked much of its effectiveness, and whose loss to the cause of missions would have been irreparable. Only a few items can be added to those already given; the rest must be gained from their excellent memoirs.

1. Ann Hasseltine, 1812-1826. Born at Bradford, Mass., December 22, 1789, her early years were marked by a restless, roving disposition; moreover she was very vivacious and intensely fond of society. When at sixteen she was converted, she threw herself with equal ardor into the service of her Master, and after graduating at Bradford, while teaching for several years, her one aim was to bring her pupils to Jesus.

In Burma she supplemented her husband's labors by studying the language of the Siamese, thousands of whom lived at Rangoon, and by translating into that tongue the Burmese Catechism, a tract, and St Matthew. She also taught schools of native girls, held women's meetings, and cultivated, for missionary reasons, the society of ladies of rank. *As sharer of her husband's imprisonment* she is best known. "She followed him from prison to prison, ministering to his wants, trying to soften the hearts of his keepers, to mitigate his sufferings, interceding with government officials or with members of the royal family. For a year and a half she thus exerted herself, walking miles in feeble health, in the darkness of the night or under a noonday sun, much of the time with a babe in her arms." When forbidden to see her husband, she would write on dough made into a cake and concealed in a bowl of rice, or send messages of affection on a roll of paper inserted in the nose of a coffeepot. The lives of others besides Dr Judson and many prison ameliorations were due to her tact and importunity. *In Amherst*, while Judson was in Ava, it was she who built their home and two schoolhouses in which she taught girls and gathered the native converts for Sabbath worship. When in her thirty-seventh year she died, with no missionary near her, after a sixteen days' illness. Burma was thus deprived of a woman of great refinement, marked intellectual power, unexampled devotion, dogged perseverance and earnest piety.

2. *Sarah Hall, 1834-1845.* She was born at Alstead, N. H., Nov. 4, 1803. From the age of ten, when she wrote a poem upon the death of Judson's first child, she had a great enthusiasm for missions. Of singular beauty, English friends declared her to be "the most finished and faultless specimen of an American woman that they had ever known." The years of wedded life made her a valued assistant of her first husband, the sainted Boardman, missionary to the Karens, and after his death she continued for

three years her important work as school teacher and itinerator through marshes and jungles and mountains. Her *schools* were so famous that later educational appropriations by the English Government stipulated that the schools should be conducted on the plan of Mrs Boardman's at Tavoy.

She was no less a treasure to Dr Judson. Her fluent *use of the Burmese*, extending even into the difficult realm of prayer, enabled her to impressively conduct women's prayer meetings and Bible classes and to translate Part I of "Pilgrim's Progress," several tracts, twenty of the best hymns, four volumes of "Scriptural Questions for Sunday-schools," and a series of Sunday cards. She likewise acquired the Peguan and superintended the translations into it of the New Testament and the best Burmese tracts. Her ability as a *writer of poetry* was above the ordinary, as is shown by her pathetic lines written shortly before her death when she expected to part from her husband at the Isle of France.

3. Emily Chubbuck, 1846-1850. She was born at Eaton, N. Y., Aug. 22, 1817, and died at Hamilton in the same state, June 1, 1854. Few American authoresses have been reared in a harder school than "*Fanny Forester*," whom Judson first met while being vaccinated at Philadelphia. The acquaintance began with his chiding her for wasting her talents on books written in a lighter vein. Her defense was that she did this as they were more salable, and it was a necessity in order to support her family. This explanation completely won his heart and he engaged her to write a life of his second wife. Before it was finished, the charmed watch which he sent her, as he had to Ann and Sarah, made her his wife, much to the scandal of the literary world, who felt that she was throwing herself away on "an old missionary," and of the friends of missions, who feared the effect of an alliance between the founder of the movement and a writer of fiction. Aside from the debt owed her for her account of Mrs Sarah Judson, she is the main source of information concerning her illustrious husband, and has given the world such missionary brilliants as "The Kathayan Slave" and "Wayside Preaching."

Judson's Private Life and Character. He was a man of large *intellectual power*, a fact evinced by his early life and by his missionary services, as well as by his contact with civilians, military men and diplomats of India, among whom he stood like a second Schwartz. Indeed, had he wished to make money and win fame, he would have accepted an important government position under the English. Marked ability of this sort is naturally accompanied by *ambition*. This striking trait of his early life remained after conversion, but was sublimated into a desire to lay foundations in new fields, to furnish a nation with a Bible, and to secure the largest possible results from the mission's work. Behind his ambition lay *a will* of singular strength backed by indomitable perseverance. A course once appearing to be pleasing to God, no temptation could turn him from it, least of all those connected with personal ease. The possible danger connected with such traits, that of self sufficiency and unwillingness to ask advice, did not injure his usefulness.

His *home life* has been very attractively described. *With his children* he was at once a mentor and a rollicking boy. His letters to them are a combination of the comic and the serious. No one of *his wives* had any reason to feel that she was anything but sole possessor of his heart, and rarely has the role of lover been prolonged with greater delicacy and sincerity. Daily walks together, little notes pinned on the curtain, to be read on awakening before his return from his morning run, bright chits scribbled surreptitiously and sent home when delayed beyond the usual time, were indications of his daily regard, while in sickness he was the nurse and health-giving sunshine.

Judson was an Israel *in prayer*. "He asked not as a duty, nor even as a pleasure, but he asked that he might receive. . . . It was a common thing for him to ask until he received, in his own consciousness, an assurance that his requests would be granted." Another writes: "His best and freest time for meditation and prayer was while walking rapidly in the open air. He, however, attended to the duty in his room, and so well was this peculiarity understood that when the children heard the somewhat long, quick, but well-measured tread up and down the room, they would say, 'Papa is praying.'" Such prayer was winged by a *sublime faith* in God. "He believed that Burma was to be converted to Christ just as much as he believed that Burma existed," and in personal need his trust was like Abraham's, reposeful as that of a child in its father's arms. His "*heavenly-mindedness*" struck every one who knew him. His earthly treasures were above, and there dwelt his Saviour and God; naturally, therefore, his conversation, and especially his hours of meditation, transported him through azure depths to heavenly mansions.

No true saint can be passive, and Judson certainly was a vigorous foe to natural sin. His ambition was curbed, his will brought into subjection to godly majorities, and growing conformity to Christ's will was attained,—but all only by a strenuous struggle and persistent trust. It occasionally went to *an ascetic extreme*, as when, after the awful strain of imprisonment and his wife's death, he gave all his property to the Board, burned up official letters of commendation, declined the degree of D. D., spent weeks among the beasts in the jungle, and like a Trappist monk, sat for hours beside a grave. Yet such times were exceptional and better circumstances gave him renewed brightness, though he never gave up the spiritual longings incited by Madame Guyon's writings.

Judson's Work. Years ago the Baptist Board testified that they had sent no missionary from this country who yielded more implicit compliance than he to all their regulations. Residents in the East testified, at the time of his death, to his remarkable ability in various spheres.

1. Relation to fellow missionaries. Some said that Judson was unsocial. As a matter of fact, his view of the value of time prevented his spending much of it in stealing that of his colleagues. It is true, also, that he strongly opposed the massing of missionaries at one point, and his uniform desire to scatter them over the field seemed to many to mark an ascetic mind. If, however, they were in affliction he was their Barnabas, and thoughtful attentions, such as securing portraits of absent children and presenting them to their parents, showed his genuine interest in them.

2. *Attitude toward the Board.* In general it was ideal; yet he often forgot that board secretaries are only the servants of a denomination,—oftentimes dead so far as missionary interest is concerned,—and his letters to them on more than one occasion are not to be imitated. Thus, his letter virtually denouncing them because they had not published the dark side of the situation abroad, would probably not have been so severe had he occupied their position. So, too, his upbraiding them for the consequences of retrenchment might have been somewhat more temperate.

3. *Intercourse with Europeans.* It is said that Judson preached but one English sermon in his thirty-seven years in Burma, though when British soldiers at Maulmain were seeking salvation, Judson ministered to them. He was naturally fond of society and proved its ornament when he could do so without neglecting his work. It was simply his whole-hearted devotion to the Burmese that caused him to abjure English preaching, teaching in English, and English reading and society. If he erred it was on the safe side of a subtle temptation. The same reason is his only justification for opposing Trevelyanism, or the Romanization of oriental tongues, which found in Duff 'so ardent an advocate.

4. *Judson and the Government.* Again and again he looked toward Ava as the only human hope for Christianity. To gain toleration he would do almost anything. So, also, he rendered valuable aid to England, with the hope that this Christian power might forward the cause. The personal salvation of rulers was constantly on his heart and to the Burman sovereign and the future king of Siam came faithful words of warning and Christian counsel. While he inculcated obedience to rulers when not involving sin, he received secret inquirers who came to him contrary to official orders.

5. *Translator and author.* Here Judson was almost peerless. His views of translation required such a reproduction of the Bible as the English Revised Version, and, thanks to such principles, rare linguistic ability, and his "lust for finishing," his Bible will long be what Luther's has been to Germany. Many missionaries have owed their rapid and accurate progress in the language to his " Gram-

matical Notices of the Burman Language,"—a marvel of campactness and lucidity,—and more still are indebted to him for his monumental dictionary. Tracts of his are not of uniform value. Thus his first one, "A View of the Christian Religion," if rendered into other tongues, would mildew in missionary book-rooms, while "The Golden Balance," written when Judson had become more Burmanized, would attract all Buddhists holding the doctrines of the "Lesser Vehicle."

6. *The itinerant.* Unwillingly Judson was compelled to forego this dangerous and fatiguing, but to him exhilarating, form of work, indulging in it only as a health-change, so to speak. He was accompanied on these tours by a number of converts, who were sent off to the right and left to meet and report to the missionary a few days later.

7. *As preacher.* Preaching was to Dr Judson a perfect delight, though much of it was conversational and before an audience of one. A most interesting picture of this latter work is given in Mrs Judson's "Wayside Preaching." In public address, "his preaching was concrete. He did not deal in vague abstractions. Truth assumed in his mind statuesque forms. . . . Behind his words when he preached lay the magnet of a great character," and native audiences were swayed by his words as the Welsh were by Christmas Evans.

8. *The pastor.* This most difficult task, involving the care of volunteer or paid assistants, was felicitously performed. He had the knack of getting the utmost out of church-members and helpers, and his wise leadership held them to him most closely. In financial matters he shrewdly managed them, giving them differing sums at irregular intervals, the total for a year being the amount voted by the Mission; but his way of dispensing it raised the recipients above mere expectant and fault-finding hirelings.

9. *Self-propagation of the work.* Judson's plan was to choose promising boys and young men and personally fit them by daily morning instruction for teachers and ministers. He also favored schools of primary or practical theological education. He writes thus upon this subject: "I am really unwilling to place young men who have just be-

gun to love their Saviour, under teachers who will strive to carry [them through a long course of study, until they are able to unravel metaphysics, and calculate eclipses, and their soul become as dry as the one and as dark as the other. . . . I want to see our young disciples thoroughly acquainted with the Bible from beginning to end, and with geography and history, so far as necessary to understand the Scriptures, and to furnish them with enlarged, enlightened minds. I would also have them carried through a course of systematic theology. . . . And I would have them well instructed in the art of communicating their ideas by word and by writing."

General Results of his Life. Did Judson turn from the attractions of the law and the drama, from an instructorship in Brown University and the wide usefulness of the "biggest church in Boston," to throw his life away as a missionary? The American and Baptist Boards, over 7000 converted Karens and Burmans gathered, at his death, into 63 churches and cared for by 163 missionaries and native assistants, a grammar and dictionary as stepping stones to early usefulness to many, leaves of life scattered widely for the healing of the nation, an entire Bible in exact and perspicuous Burmese, streams of influence reaching out into Siam and even to the Jews, a stalwart character moulded by Christ, and a perennial example of devotion to the "Greatest Work in the World," left to all the church —all of these either partially or wholly the fruitage of that magnificent "throwing away," are a convincing reply.

SUGGESTED READINGS.

Conant: The Earnest Man, (1856), Chs. xiv-xxvi.
Dowling: The Judson Offering, (1847), Pp. 45-294.
Eddy: The Three Mrs Judsons, (1860), Pp. 207-233, 251-270.
Encyclopædia of Missions, (1891), Articles Adoniram, Sarah H. and Emily C. Judson.
Hervey: The Story of Baptist Missions, (1884), Chs xiv-xvii.
Johnston: Life of Adoniram Judson, (1887), Chs. viii-xx.
Edward Judson: Notable Baptists: Adoniram Judson, (1894), Chs. vi-xiii.

Mrs E. C. Judson: Sarah Boardman, (1848).
Kendrick: Emily Chubbuck Judson, (1860). Especially Chs. XIV-XXVI.
Knowles: Ann Hasseltine Judson (1835), Chs VIII-XVIII.
Missionary Review of the World, April, 1894, Pp. 259-261.
Page: Noble Workers, (1875), Pp. 209-224.
Piper and Maccracken: Lives of the Leaders of Our Church Universal, (1879), Pp. 842-849.
Pitman: Heroines of the Mission Field, Pp. 96-122.
Richards: Adoniram Judson, the Apostle of Burma, (an Epic, 1889), Pp. 19-103.
Stuart: Lives of the three Mrs Judsons, (1851), Pp. 183-356.
Thomson: Great Missionaries, (1862), Pp. 291-298.
Vanguard of the Christian Army, Pp. 87-132.
Walsh: Modern Heroes of the Mission Field, (1882), Pp. 75-94.
Wayland: Memoir of Rev. Dr. Judson, (1853), Vol. I., Pp. 178 to end of Vol. II.; especially I., Chs. x., XIII., and II., Chs. II., III., VI.-X.
Wyeth: Missionary Memorials: Sarah B. and Emily C. Judson, (1894).
Yonge: Pioneers and Founders, (1890), Pp 129-171.
Young: Modern Missions and Their Triumphs, (1888), Pp. 79-89.
Edward Judson: The Life of Adoniram Judson, (1883). Life in Rangoon, Ch. VI.; Life in Ava and Oung-pen-la, Ch. VII.; Life in Amherst and Maulmain, Chs. VIII-X.; Visit to America, Ch. XI.; Last Years, Ch. XII.; Posthumous Influence, Ch. XIII.

III

DUFF'S EARLY LIFE AND EDUCATIONAL WORK

That tall figure, crossing the street and looking thoughtfully to the ground, stooped somewhat in the shoulders and his hand awkwardly grasping the lappet of his coat, is Alexander Duff, the pride of the college, whose mind has received the impress of Chalmers' big thoughts and the form of his phraseology. Under Chalmers, he was, in St Andrews, the institutor of Sabbath-schools and the originator of the Students' Missionary Society.—*Rev J. W. Taylor*, of Flisk.

Early Years. Almost at the geographical center of Scotland, the home of great missionaries, lies the little town of Moulin, near which was born on the twenty-fifth of April, 1806, Alexander Duff, one of the foremost apostles of this century. Scott calls Perthshire, in which Moulin is situated, "the fairest portion of the northern kingdom," a claim made good by its forests and fertile straths, its rivers and lakes, mountains and glens. And that eighty by seventy mile shire was full of worthy memories also; for did it not contain the Killiecrankie, Tippermuir and Sheriffmuir battlefields? and did it not possess memorials of Bruce and Queen Mary and Rob Roy as well as boast of connections in Scott and Wordsworth? Of this home shire Duff writes in later years: "Amid scenery of unsurpassed beauty and grandeur, I acquired early tastes and impulses which have animated and influenced me through life."

James Duff and Jean Rattray. James Duff, was it is true, a
    "dalesman, child of rock and stream;"
but he was as much more as Carlyle's father was more than a mere stonemason. He and Jean before their marriage were electrified by the new spiritual life brought one com-

munion Sabbath into their services by the sainted Charles Simeon, who had come up from the house top overlooking the beautiful Backs between King's College and the river Cam, and who changed their pastor into an evangelical leaven. When Duff visited Cambridge many years after, he enjoyed a long interview with this evangelical Anglican, whom he considered his spiritual ancestor.

While his mother's early influence was much valued, Duff wrote in later years of the powerful effect exerted upon his life by *his father*. His Sabbath-schools and the weekly meetings at his own home, when his Scripture expositions and rapturous prayers carried the hearer to the very gates of heaven, his peculiar power of winning the young through the picturing of Bible truth, and especially the moving manner in which he set forth the bleeding, dying love of the Saviour, ineffaceably impressed themselves on his son. James Duff was, in turn, held by the spell of his reconverted pastor's spirit and by the silent fellowship of the old divines whose works contain the "sap and marrow of the gospel" and were fragrant with "the flavor of Paradise." The influence of such a father is thus testified to: "In the sharpness and clearness with which he drew the line between the merely expedient and the absolutely right and true; in his stern adhesion to principle at all hazards; in his ineffable loathing for temporizing and compromise, in any shape or form, where the interest of 'Zion's King and Zion's cause' were concerned; in his energy of spirit, promptness of decision, and unbending sturdihood of character; in the Abraham-like cast of his faith, which manifested itself in its directness, simplicity and strength,—in all these and other respects he always appeared to me to realize fully as much of my own beau-ideal of the ancient martyr or hero of the Covenant as any other man I ever knew. . . . Oh that a double portion of his spirit were mine, and that the mantle of his graces would fall upon me!" .

Duff's Education. As the Moulin "dominie" spent more time on watch-repairing and fishing than on instructing the school children, Alexander was sent at the early age of eight to a better school between Dunkeld and Perth. Three years there prepared him for the Kirkmichael school, whose reputation commended it to his father. He had the good fortune to live under the roof of its accomplished master, Mr Macdougall, and to count among his schoolfellows some prominent men of a later day. Duff as *dux* of the school was put forward on state occasions to read the Odes of Horace, and left it to afterward exclaim, "What would I have been this day, had not an overruling Providence directed me to Kirkmichael school?" Another year at Perth Grammar School, where he was again *dux*, had much to do with his later educational work, as he here came under the influence of a born teacher, Mr Moncur. This man's first act as master was to summon the janitor and bid him sink in the Tay the entire outfit of torturing tawse, after which "he asked why the generous youths entrusted to him should be treated as savages." This was the germ of Duff's Indian school management and the animus lying behind the address "To the Native Gentlemen of Calcutta" who had in their hatred conspired to kill him.

At St. Andrews, Scotland's most venerable University, Alexander was entered at fifteen. In spite of its bleakness and the hermit-like isolation of its students, the future missionary received here the strongest impulses of his life. It was not so much the fact that he sat at the feet of men like Dr Hunter, the Latinist, and Dr Jackson, the scientist, nor that he came off with the highest honors in Greek, Latin, logic and natural philosophy, as it was contact with one of the greatest of his countrymen, which made St Andrews his Arabia. The captivating eloquence of Chalmers, the advent of a man of genius whose presence was a liberal education in itself, and the delightful freshness of his spiritual life as it emptied itself into the Dead Sea of formal religion, were epoch-making elements in the life of all the students. Coming from the wynds of Glasgow and his miracle-working there, Duff was inspired to do like him, and so organized Sabbath-schools and private circles for Bible study. Before leaving the University, Duff could say: " I have personally visited all the lower classes in town, and did not find twenty children who were not attending some school or other."

Other Educational Influences than those named were almost equally helpful. Books were the delight of his heart. In childhood the "Cloud of Witnesses" with which his father saturated his mind, the "Day of Judgment" and "The Skull" of Dugald Buchanan, a Perthshire Ossian, filled him with mingled emotions of hatred and awe. When at fifteen he left the Grammar School of Perth, he carried with him Johnson's "Rambler" and, more important still, a pocket copy of "Paradise Lost," the daily reading of which unconsciously brought into his thought and modes of expression their formative power. Thus there entered into his fibre the elements so prominent in his life,—"the Gaelic Buchanan and the English Milton, the Celtic fire and the Puritan imagination, feeding on Scripture story and classic culture, colored by such dreams and experiences, and directed by such a father and teacher."

The Missionary Call. The *dreams* above alluded to, were in a sense the precursors of his missionary decision. The first vision was a personal rendering of Buchanan's "Latha Bhreitheanais" in which he stood before the Judge at the Last Day. The effect was such that it evoked an earnest cry for pardon and led to an assurance of forgiveness through the blood of Jesus. The second was a more direct intimation of the will of God, who descended in a heavenly chariot and called to the Scotch laddie sleeping in the blae-berries by the burn side, "Come up hither; I have work for thee to do." His *father's teachings* were decidedly missionary in their tone. "Pictures of Jugganath and other heathen idols he was wont to exhibit accompanying the exhibition with copious explanations, well fitted to create a feeling of horror towards idolatry and of compassion towards the poor blinded idolaters, and intermixing the whole with statements of the love of Jesus."

When in St Andrews this childish interest broadened under the missionary enthusiasm of Dr Chalmers, and through the friendship of students like Urquhart, his roommate. They and others organized the Students' Missionary Society, Duff being librarian. Their object was to study foreign missions with the purpose of learning of the needs of the non-Christian world, Chalmers abetting their efforts by a monthly lecture on missions in the town-hall. The society was the parent of the most famous missionaries of the country. Marshman and Yates from India and Morrison with his story of China, added their quota by firing the men with apostolic zeal. Duff not only succeeded in getting missionary books read by others; he also read much himself and it was when he had perused the elaborate article, "India," in Brewster's "Edinburgh Encyclopædia," that his soul first felt the fascinating spell of a land that was to bind itself around his whole being.

As the Established Church of Scotland had no missionaries in any field,—in spite of the motto of the first Confession, "And this glaid tydingis of the kyngdome sall be precheit through the haill warld for a witnes unto all natiouns, and then sall the end cum,"—the interest thus aroused seemed likely to be ineffective. But the spirit of missions was abroad and the Church awoke. Dr Inglis at home and Dr Bryce in Calcutta had brought the General Assembly in 1824 to agree to establish in India an educational work, and in 1828 Duff was asked to head the enterprise. How the young student met the question is seen in letters written to Dr Chalmers and to other friends. He counts the cost and after deliberately weighing the cons and pros he feels the weight of the latter and writes: "May the former considerations not only be weakened, but be utterly swept out of existence. O Lord, I feel their littleness, their total insignificancy, and for the sake of promoting Thy glory among the heathen, I cordially, cheerfully embrace the latter: yea, if such were thy will, I am ready to go to the parched desert or the howling wilderness, to live on its bitter herbs and at the mercy of its savage inhabitants."

He had *decided this important matter alone;* for he concluded that the present inquiry rested almost solely between himself and his Maker. His *fathers' disappointment* and objections were answered from his own statements when dealing with missions as an abstract matter, and he begins to pray that his son may approve himself not merely a common soldier of the cross, but a champion. Duff overcomes his *mother's natural affection* thus:

"Beware of making an idol of me. While you feel all the tenderness of parental love, . . . be earnest in prayer to God that Satan may not tempt you to raise me to an undue place in your affections, lest God, in his holy displeasure, see fit to remove me not only to India, but to the land of skulls and sepulchres. Think then, ponder, pray over these things, and may God Himself guide and direct you into the ways of peace and heavenly resignation." But the matter had its exalted aspects, and his letters, as also his addresses, picture the lofty vocation of the missionary, and parents and audiences forgot the sacrifice in the exceeding weight of glory.

Preparation for Departure. Quaint Patrick Lawson, whom Duff used to visit annually for the sake of his "rich and racy biblical talk," abruptly asked him one day whether he intended to marry. His negative reply elicited some sage advice: "Be quietly on the look out; and if in God's providence, you make the acquaintance of one of the daughters of Zion, traversing, like yourself, the wilderness of this world, her face set thitherward, get into friendly converse with her." The old Bunyan's counsel was acted upon, and in Edinburgh he found such a person in *Anne Scott Drysdale*, of whom Dr Smith writes: "Never had even missionary a more devoted wife. Sinking herself in her husband from the very first, she gave him a new strength, and left the whole fulness of his nature and his time free for the one work of his life."

Conference with gentlemen who had been in India, studying the religion and character of the Hindus, inspecting the best conducted schools in the Scotch Athens, and conferring with the Committee who had the Indian Mission in charge, filled his days before sailing. The ordination trials over and Dr Chalmer's eloquent ordination sermon delivered, he and his wife sailed in October in the "Lady Holland." As the result of his own preference and the ignorance of the Committee, he went forth with no restrictions save one —which he disregarded soon after he reached India—and so was free to do what his good judgment dictated.

"In Perils of Waters." Just off the English coast, they encountered a derelict, which proved a true omen of the voyage. While taking on a cargo at Madeira, a storm drove the ship to sea. A three weeks' delay gave Duff opportunity to look about the island and also to do some preaching. Re-embarking, they were saved from pirates by the presence of a frigate. Driven almost to the coast of South America, they finally were just about rounding the Cape of Good Hope, when in a heavy sea and in the darkness the ship ran on the rocks off Dassen Island. The excitement was intense and it was then that the effect of Duff's preaching and daily morning worship became evident. Through exciting experiences all were landed on a penguin island by daybreak, and soon thereafter they were rescued by a brig of war sent from Cape Town. The *incident which most affected Duff's future* in connection with this wreck was the destruction of his entire library of eight hundred volumes, with the sole exception of his Bagster's Bible and a Psalter, which were picked up by a sailor uninjured though wet. His journals, notes, essays and memoranda—the harvesting of his student days—were also lost and all this produced in him the conviction that "human learning must be to him a means only, not in itself an end."

Once again on the ocean, they were no less unfortunate. Beaten out of their course, overcome almost by a hurricane when off Mauritius, they finally reached the banks of the Hooghly only to become the victims of a cyclone which *a second time wrecked* them. A merciful deliverance brought them to the land and to a heathen temple, where they were allowed to rest, as they were not received in the homes of the caste-ridden inhabitants. From this place of discomfort they were soon removed to Calcutta, where they were hospitably received and early met the principal residents, both missionary and diplomatic.

The Calcutta of 1830. This tall and handsome man of twenty-four, "with flashing eye, quivering voice, and restless gesticulation, . . . heir of Knox and Chalmers, had to begin in the heart of Hinduism what they had carried out in the mediævalism of Rome and the moderatism of the Kirk of the eighteenth century." What were the conditions obtaining when he began his work in India?

Strange to say, no one was able to accurately tell him. Merchants and government officials were intent on one thing, the securing at the earliest moment of a competency enabling them to return home; and hence their knowledge of the city and its inhabitants was gained in their offices or stores and in their daily drive on The Course. The missionaries there had never fully defined the situation, but Duff accompanied them everywhere, watching them deal with the natives under most diverse circumstances. Moreover, he made friends with merchants, zemindars, rajahs and Brahmans, and from native lips, through English and Bengali, learned the problems which he must meet.

Calcutta then had a population of about half a million while within a radius of ten miles was an estimated one of two millions. Within the city were many *young men who wished to learn English*, largely as a stepping stone to mercantile or governmental employment. To meet this need and higher objects, adventurers, Eurasians and Armenians had given instruction mainly in the language alone. In 1817 David Hare and the famous Rammohun Roy established the first English seminary in India, "The Hindoo College of Calcutta." This had lost all its capital soon after Duff's arrival, and the Calcutta School Society, associated with it and intolerant of Christianity, had perished. Measures providing for useful education and calculated also to "raise the moral character of those who partake of its advantages," were proposed by the directors of the East India Company, but when the medium of instruction was discussed, an angry struggle took place between the advocates of Sanskrit for the Hindus and Arabic and Persian for Muhammadans, and those who desired to use English as the sole medium for higher education.

Missionaries outside the city had advocated a Christian and English higher education before Duff's advent, but in the capital itself little Christian and educational work had been accomplished. Sati, infanticide, the choking of the dying with sacred mud, idolatry, caste, human sacrifice and thuggery still flourished. Though The Baptist, Orissa General Baptist, Church and London Missionary Societies were laboring there, *three years before his coming* there were only fifteen converts in the city as the result of ten years' work, while not more than five thousand children were in school. When he landed, "not more than five hundred of these learned English, and that after the straitest sect of secularists of the Tom Paine stamp."

Duff's Educational Plan. *Negatively* it was two-fold, not to do as the Home Committee had directed him, and not to imitate his predecessors in India. This decision would seem presumptuous in the extreme, were it not supported by such exhaustive and conclusive reasoning as may be found in "India and Indian Missions" and by the unanwerable argument of later results.

He states it *positively* and germinally in these words: "While you engage in directly separating as many precious atoms from the mass as the stubborn resistance to ordinary appliances can admit, we shall, with the blessing of God, devote our time and strength to the preparing of a mine, and the setting up of a train which shall one day explode and tear up the whole from its lowest depths." More specifically:

1. The object of Duff's educational project was to forward in the best way the accomplishment of three aims: preaching to adults; educating the young; furnishing a Bible and suitable literature. Fully educated natives seemed to him the key to the problem, and his institutions were to furnish these.

2. The kind of school best fitted to do such work was one of high grade, but as raw material was at first lacking, he was obliged to begin with a lower class of work.

3. The place for such a plant was then Calcutta, since it met best his three conditions,—a dense population from which to draw pupils, a desire on the part of many of these people to avail themselves of western learning, and the absence of hostile prepossessions against European supervision. Moreover, Calcutta was then the skull of India, and its brain, rather than its heart, was what he aimed to win.

4. Pupils were to be drawn from every class, provided they showed the proper ability and docility; but Duff preferred to receive those of higher rank or caste, believing that if he could raise up one Knox he would be worth ten thousand illiterate peasants. Brahmans, so rarely sought by other missionaries, he looked upon with special favor for this reason.

5. *Medium of instruction.* No man believed more than he in the value of the vernacular. Every student of his must know it well; but for advanced studies he boldly and contrary to government opinion and missionary usage, decided upon the English. *Bengali* was objectionable in that experiment had shown that it was impossible to keep students longer in such schools than was sufficient to get a mere smattering of an education. Such schools, moreover, attracted a poorer class of students, who were not potentially so valuable to India. Again, Bengali was the language of neither law nor religion and its terminology was too meager to serve as a vehicle of western thought, even if it possessed such books. *Sanskrit* was not chosen for the following among other reasons : it was not so perfect an instrument for conveying European knowledge; it was more difficult for the student to acquire than English; being considered divine, three-fourths of the people were forbidden to learn it; hardly any European works were translated into it; its terminology carried with it superstitious or false ideas. The very process of learning English, on the other hand, brought in with the new terms new ideas and truths, and opened up to the student an unsurpassed literature.

6. *The studies* pursued were to be first the Bible,— every student having some Bible work each day,—and then every variety of useful knowledge, first in elementary forms, but later ascending to all branches of western culture. In all these studies religion was to be the animating spirit.

7. *The method of instruction* was then new in mission schools. It was in accordance with the "Intellectual System" and is practically the method pursued in our best public schools of to-day. The alphabet was taught to classes, even this work being made a keen intellectual contest. "Instructors," prepared by Duff and used for several decades thereafter, carried the student by logical and simple steps from point to point until he could study western text-books as readily as students in our colleges.

8. The beginning of this work occurred July 13, 1830, less than seven weeks after his arrival. In a hall secured for him by Rammohun Roy, five young men recommended by him appeared. The plan as laid before them, approved itself to them and to their friends, so that in three days one hundred and five were enrolled. Expecting to classify these on the following day, he was prevented by the appearance of two hundred new applicants. As the hall accommodated but one hundred and twenty,—later, accommodations for two hundred and fifty were secured,—and as the number of candidates increased during the next week, Duff was able to sift his students and to secure a written promise from parents that they would pay for the books used and would see that their sons were present punctually and for a prolonged period, thus doing away with the instability of other mission schools.

When the institution thus organized was *formally opened* and the students were asked to read in the Bible, there was danger of a revolt; but the counsel of India's Erasmus, Rammohun Roy,—himself a student of the Bible in its original tongues,—and Duff's matchless persuasiveness, won the day, as was also the case when the Lord's prayer was first used. Lack of qualified teachers, habits of lawlessness, absence of thought so common to rote students, had to be met, but St Andrews' first scholar, debater and essayist was equal to the labor. Possibly no missionary teacher has so enthused and re-created oriental students in a year as did he. The result of a public exhibition of the work done by them in a twelvemonth was the only thing talked about in Calcutta for days thereafter, and Duff had at a bound passed from his Rubicon to the chair of dictator in the realm of missionary education, though Pompey was still unconquered.

9. Some other results may be noted. Of Duff's first students one-fourth were Brahmans and there were very few of low caste. These young men were being daily influenced to give up their false beliefs, no matter whether the impulse came from the first two English letters and word learned, o–x, ox, or from the reading of Paul's Canticle of Love. Naturally the cry of "Hinduism in Danger!" followed and chronic boycotts, succeeded by greater triumphs, were experienced. In spite of opposition Duff soon had the joy of seeing four converts, one of them an exceedingly influential Brahman.

A wider work was also being accomplished. Duff's object lesson had given birth to scores of somewhat similar seminaries, whose duly qualified teachers were in many cases his own students. Sir Charles Trevelyan had not been a week in Calcutta when, in 1831, he threw himself into Duff's ranks. His talented brother-in-law, Macaulay, was the Law Member of the Council a little later, and he, too, felt the spell of the young Scotchman. These three men were nobly backed by Lord William Bentinck and the result of the agitation was *the decree of 1835*, in which the Governor-General sanctions in the Government institutions Duff's system almost in its entirety, though lacking its religious element. One year afterwards the Government English schools were doubled in number. Sir Charles later attributed much of this Renaissance to him, while a prominent Indian writer says that Macaulay's greatest work— greater even than his Warren Hastings and Clive essays, —" was to be the legislative completion of the young Scottish missionary's policy."

SUGGESTED READINGS.

Catholic Presbyterian, Article Alexander Duff, Vol. III.; Pp. 215 ff.

Duff: India and Indian Missions, (1840), Chs. IV, VI.

W. P. Duff: Memorials of Alexander Duff, D.D.

Encyclopædia of Missions, (1891), Article Alexander Duff.

Free Church Record, April, 1878, Pp. 95, 96.

Good Words, Article Educational Work of Duff, Vol XIX., Pp 307 ff.

Lal Behari Day: Recollections of Alexander Duff, D.D., LL.D., (1879), Chs. I-IV.

Pierson: New Acts of the Apostles, (1894), Pp. 128-132.

T. Smith: Alexander Duff, D.D., LL. D., (1883), Chs. I-III.

Vermilye: The Life of Alexander Duff, (1890), Chs. I-IV.

G. Smith: The Life of Alexander Duff, D. D. LL. D., (1879). The Boy and Student, Vol. I., Ch. I.; The First Missionary of the Church of Scotland, Vol. I., Ch. II.; The Two Shipwrecks, Vol. I., Ch. III.; Calcutta as it Was, Vol. I., Ch. IV.; Beginning of the Work, Vol. I., Chs. V, VI.; The Renaissance in India, Vol. I., Chs. VII, VIII.; Work for Eurasians, Native Christians and Europeans, Vol, I., Ch. IX.

IV

DUFF AS A PROMOTER OF MISSIONS

Wherever I wander, wherever I stay, my heart is in India, in deep sympathy with its multitudinous inhabitants, and in earnest longings for their highest welfare in time and in eternity.—Duff's latest published words.

Other Labors in India, 1830-1834. Jungle-fever, contracted during a journey to Takee to inspect his branch school, followed by dysentery, almost as fatal as cholera before ipecacuanha had been used as a specific against it, gave Duff a much regretted furlough. Yet in these four years in India he had accomplished much. Besides the central work already mentioned, he had delivered lectures which set the young mind of India thinking on religious topics; in their debating societies and elsewhere he had agitated the establishment of a national system of female education; India's first modern medical school, grown to be the largest in the world, came into existence largely because of testimony before the Educational Committee given by Duff and his Brahman pupils, who had so imbibed his spirit that they were ready to commit the awful sacrilege of dissecting a human body; the germ of the Doveton Colleges, so helpful to despised Eurasians, was nourished by their best friend, Duff; he had proposed his masterly scheme for a United Christian College, later realized in Madras for Southern India, but foolishly and expensively rejected at this time because of English sectarian controversy; his appeal for vernacular education, so sadly needed by ninety-two per cent. of the children of Bengal, required for its continual agitation a free organ of expression, and so the "Calcutta Christian Observer" had come to birth; Trevelyanism, or the Romanization of East Indian languages,—numbering two hundred and forty-three plus a larger number of dialects,—was so dependent upon him that its author, Sir Charles, writes: "The turning point of the controversy was marked by the publication of three papers by Dr Duff, in the first of which the possibility, practicability and expediency of substituting the Roman for the Indian alphabet was discussed, and in the last two a practical scheme for that purpose was worked out in detail, and objections were answered. . . . They settled the system on its present basis, and may be read to this day with interest and advantage."

From his part in this controversy and his roll of champion of the Anglicists, we must not imagine that he was opposed to true oriental scholarship and the cultivation of the vernacular in higher education. *Bengali received its greatest impulse* at that time from Duff's institution, where the despised language was enriched from contact with western thought and was systematically cultivated in the interests of Bengal's evangelization. In regard to Orientalism, *all that Duff criticised and opposed was a pseudo-Orientalism*, which failed to see all that was valuable in such literature, and yet stoutly argued that government money should be expended on costly works in oriental tongues which it was necessary to pay men to learn to read. Moreover, he felt that a worse wrong had been done India than that of waste; heathenism had been endowed, while Christianity had been set back by such action. The folly of Orientalism, such as was shown in the medical college controversy, was also opposed. His high appreciation of a true oriental scholarship is set forth in one of the finest paragraphs of his valuable pamphlet, the "New Era of the English language and English Literature in India."

But the man had been *more directly working for Christianity* also. He was a staunch and aggressive worker in the line of Bible and Tract distribution. When the first writ of *habeas corpus* was served and the character of missionaries was in consequence assailed, the Highlander, rather than the Bishop of Calcutta, came to the rescue. *St Andrew's Kirk*, the official "cathedral" of the Scotch, was in bad repute. Legal wars had been carried on between its chaplain and the Bishop of Calcutta, concerning a steeple first, then over its weather-cock, and last of all concerning a second service argued for by the junior chaplain. As a result it had lost its members and was a scandal to Christianity. Dr Bryce, returning to Scotland, threw the care of this church on Duff, thus giving to the city such preaching as it had never heard before. A happy sequel to his labors there was his admonition to one of his parishoners, an employer of five hundred natives, who allowed them to *work on Sundays*, as was common at that time. The result of this advice was the payment of Sunday wages without requiring its work to those who would make their labor on other days more profitable. Thus what a bishop had failed to do through a pledge to abstain from Sabbath desecration, was done by the quiet advice of a missionary, and Sabbath keeping began.

Before setting sail on the " John M'Lellan," Alexander Duff had seen all these forces in motion and his beloved institution had become *"a complete Arts College*, including the thorough study of the Bible as well as the evidences and doctrines of natural and revealed religion," the annual examinations of which were among the notable events of the year. What larger work can any young man of twenty-eight hope to accomplish?

Five years in Britain, 1835-1839. During the voyage the convalescent improved the opportunity thus afforded by reading the entire Bible through three times. The result of this comparative and repeated study was an enthusiastic conviction that " missionary work is merely preparatory to the great outpouring of the Holy Spirit." He did one other thing of importance on the journey; he outlined a plan for reaching every presbytery with the missionary message. To us this seems commonplace, but Dr Chalmers gives him the credit of being the first man to present personally a cause in such a manner. Of the many results of this stay in the home-land, only three are here named.

1. Results coming from *missionary oratory*. In this direction Dr Duff has probably had no equal, either in Europe or America. Received coldly by the Committee on his

return, he was first *called sternly to account* for presenting his work before some friends in a private house. The Convener's censure was promptly turned into victory and the Scotch of *London* wished to hear him. He had scarcely made a beginning there when his old enemy, jungle-fever, laid him low. But *the General Assembly of 1835* was soon to meet in Edinburgh's box-like Tron Church, and he felt that he must be heard there or die. The opportunity being given Duff—who was just off from a sick-bed and spoke against the advice of his physician,—he arose, and after passing beyond the stage when his friends felt that he would drop to the floor, gave utterance to a flood of oratory which furnished to schools and elocutionary manuals for many years one of their best models. For between two and three hours he held the vast audience captive beneath his commanding eloquence. Callous lawyers and lords of session, churchmen and laity of every degree, were moved to tears, and when the tumult of emotion had subsided, the venerable Dr Stewart said: "Moderator, it has been my privilege to hear Mr Fox and Mr Pitt speak in the House of Commons, that grand focus of British eloquence, when in the very zenith of their glory as statesmen and orators. I now solemnly declare that I never heard from either of them a speech similar or second to that to which we have now listened, alike for its lofty tone, thought and sentiment, its close argumentative force, its transcending eloquence and overpowering impressiveness." At one blow he had struck off the locks of heretofore unwilling church doors and every one wished to hear this new Chrysostom. Twenty thousand copies of his speech published by the Assembly's order, as well as almost every newspaper in the realm, scattered broadcast the masterful oration.

Read to-day, it cannot produce the impression originally felt. We live in the age of knowledge, and missionary addresses are not the novelty that they were then. Notwithstanding, one reading now the ruins of that production, and especially its peroration, is stirred with the grandeur of his theme,—India, India for Christ, India through the Christian use of education, and all this the privilege of godly Scotland! His blood-earnestness, due to agonizing prayer like that of Knox, save that he longed that God would give him India; periods unconsciously molded in the form of early favorites of his, Chatham, Burke, Erskine and Canning; his prophet-like utterance and utter disregard of modern laws of elocution; the impression given that he was the spokesman of his Master in behalf of perishing millions; the final supernatural effect produced by his whispered peroration: these are some of the *points which struck the hearer most forcibly*. And other notable efforts, like that at London and his famous Vindication of the Mission at the Assembly of 1837, were marked by similar traits, though he later made a more liberal use of satire than in his first address.

If one proof of the Athenian orator's power was the cry, "Let us go against Philip!" *Duff was a Demosthenes;* for an Act was passed recommending him to the churches and advising that in each congregation an agency for prayer and the propagation of missionary intelligence be created. Less pleasant results were calls extended to him from churches of various degrees, including the famous Greyfriars, and urgent requests that he give up India. It pained him that people should even suppose that he would "retreat from the front of the battle into the easy and yet respectable comfort of the baggage." Aberdeen honored itself and him by conferring the degree of D. D., and this to a man under thirty in a land where the letters are more than "semi-lunar fardels" and are never carelessly bestowed.

2. *As an organizer*, even more satisfactory results were secured. From the Orkneys to Solway Firth there was no considerable district which he did not visit and organize, so far as possible, the presbyteries and churches into missionary branches of the foreign work. The first Ladies' Society in Scotland and its imitators were due to him. Financial aid to the missionary work of the Church increased fourteen fold during the years that this Celtic firebrand flamed on Scotia's hills.

The result which seemed to him personally the most important, was *the securing of strong recruits*. His own strength and the large results of his four years in India drew to him some of the choicest men from the Universities,—

John Anderson of Madras, and Doctors Mitchell and Smith, who were to become so powerful in India, as well as those almost-persuaded men who remained behind to hold the ropes, such as the sainted McCheyne and the talented Guthrie. Instead of being the Church of Scotland's sole representative as in 1830, when he was ready to return, eight others were there laboring; the Church had in its hands his "Vindication," which demanded of the Assembly that they send out to races like the Hindus their best educated ministers and ablest preachers; and divinity students the world over had material for serious meditation in his most popular writing, "Missions the Chief end of the Christian Church; also the Qualifications, Duties and Trials of an Indian Missionary."

Back to Calcutta, 1839, 1840. Duff's journey to India was a profitable one to him. Going by the Overland Route, he was delayed *in Egypt for a month*. Besides reviewing the remains of a mighty Empire, he sought an interview with the Patriarch of the Coptic Church, being anxious to see if "life could be breathed into the shriveled skeleton of so fruitful and so noble a mother of churches." The Patriarch listened with interest to suggestions concerning the use of the Bible and the publication of tracts, and when an institution for higher education was broached the old man assented and asked Mr Lieder, the missionary accompanying him, to draft a plan for his more careful inspection. Duff's desire has since been partly accomplished by the noble efforts of American missionaries. The cornerstone of the first English Church in Alexandria, on its great square, was about to be laid, and Dr Duff performed the religious part of the ceremonies. Later this child of the Covenant and lover of Ben Nevis, went into the *solitudes of Sinai* for a fortnight. Conversing with the monks of St Catherine's Convent through Hindustani, confirming his own faith through a careful study of the topography of the mountain, which could be touched as his own Grampians could not, ascending the peak where Moses stood when the Divine Law was given him, he repeats many times on a Sabbath day the Ten commandments and luxuriates in a flood of sublime and spiritual reflections.

The Suez steamer came early in February, 1840, and the Duffs duly reached *Bombay*, where they enjoyed the fellowship of their fellow missionaries, the famous John Wilson, Robert Nesbit, his old St Andrew's fellow worker, and Murray Mitchell, one of his Scotland recruits. Duff comforted them in the misfortunes attending their first Parsi conversions, and made a careful study of the conditions in western India. Thence they took a teak-built vessel to Calcutta, stopping on the way at *Mangalore*,—where a visit with the eccentric Basel missionary, Hebich, kept Duff talking until almost dawn, and at *Madras* where were their own recruits, Anderson and Johnson. The interest taken by Duff in the conversion of old St Andrews school into the germs of what is to-day the great Christian College of Madras, and in John Anderson,—who with John Wilson at Bombay and himself at Calcutta constituted the basal triangle of missionary educational work in India,—was great and fruitful. Later they sail for the Hooghly, where a May cyclone again almost destroys them.

Second Stadium in India, 1840-1850. The first decade of his missionary life had laid down the lines which he afterward followed; hence his later years can be passed over more rapidly.

Duff had hardly had time to look about him *on landing* and note English signs of native druggists and surgeons, a beautiful Gothic church presided over by a high caste Brahman brought to Christ from atheism through his efforts, and the magnificent college buildings and mission house where he was to live surrounded by nearly seven hundred enthusiastic pupils, before he found himself plunged into a *conflict with the Governor-General*, Lord Auckland. In his absence, the liberties fought for by himself and others, which resulted in the use of the English tongue and the study of western science in public institutions of learning, had been taken away and given to the Orientalists, and error was again endowed. In three bold letters he arraigns his Lordship at the bar of universal reason and before the Judge of Lords. While the letters availed nothing, another protest against the public support of heathenism and a plea for a Christian education had been uttered.

Though the institution under its four gifted colleagues had made great progress, it was ripe for a *reorganization* looking toward the one spiritual end of the conversion of students, the ultimate overthrow of the Brahmanical system and the substitution of a self-propagating native Church. While at home he had been a student of the latest educational ideas, and to his buildings, library and apparatus, he now proceeded by a normal class and by privately training those already acting as instructors in the college, to raise up a body of thoroughly trained teachers,—an attempt so successful that the Government and missions from Burma to Sindh speedily carried off his graduates. Note-books were discouraged and Duff aimed to get into his students' minds clear and correct conceptions with the ability to express them.

For three years he held a Sunday *class for Bible study* among the clerks in public offices, with encouraging spiritual results. For his *old graduates* who desired the elevating companionship and intellectual stimulus of their old instructor, Duff held a week-day evening lecture, when works of men like Guizot and John Foster were discussed. Older and *less favored men* were aided by weekly lectures on moral and religious themes. The woes of child-marriage and widowhood made an appeal to his vigorous pen. The Krishnaghur movement and its sect of Worshippers of the Creator so interested him that he investigated the matter, and *two new stations* were added to Takee. Meanwhile at the college most of the time of the missionaries was spent in teaching, conversing, preaching, translating, preparing tracts and praying together, while Duff's nine hundred students were receiving at their hands a thorough and Christian training.

The Disruption of 1843, though it was not unexpected, was a terrible blow to Duff when it came. While at home he had claimed that missions lay outside the realm of party, but with the formation of the Free Church, he and his colleagues felt that they must cast in their lot with the off-shoot. This meant the giving up of an institution finely equipped, much of it with his own private means, to the Established Church and the beginning over again, with little hope of assistance from a struggling church at home. But Dr Duff was master of the hour in India. Friends were raised up and in 1844 a hall devoted to idol revelries was secured and the new institution began with a thousand pupils. His magnanimity forbade his starting a work too near his old institution; hence this less central heathen hall. Similarly a man who could move all Calcutta by his "Voice from the Ganges,"—four lectures given in the town hall on the reasons for separating from the Established Church,—had little difficulty in building a church for the members of the new denomination, and when it fell down, he speedily raised twice as much for a new one costing $60,000.

Other efforts of this period were the development of the branch schools, by which natives were evangelizing the rural districts; the editorship of the liberal "Calcutta Review" of which he was one of the three founders,—a thesaurus of valuable information concerning India;—a sermon preached after the deadly summer of 1844, which partly accounts for the largest single hospital in the world and the ten others which later followed; and raising money for a Knox monument in Edinburgh and again for starving Highlanders.

Personal matters were the attempt to kill one whose Institution was turning out Christian graduates to the threatened subversion of Hinduism,—an attempt met by his tactful letter and turned to his advantage,—and the crushing intelligence of the *death of Thomas Chalmers*, whose successor he was strenuously urged to become. In spite of appeals from presbyteries and the General Assembly itself, Duff resolutely turned from so great an honor that he might "retain in the view of all men, the clearly marked and distinguishing character of a missionary to the heathen abroad,"—a conclusion which gave the utmost joy to all classes of the Indian community, not excluding the Brahmans, whose appeal is a strange commentary on Duff's fascinating power and on Brahmanical inconsistency. While his colleagues agreed that he ought not to desert India, they thought it wise for him to return and organize the Free Church Mission scheme. Dr Duff yielded to their views as well as to those of his physician and after a most interesting tour through India, that he might know the situation and drink in inspiration from the haunts of men whose life stirred his blood, he embarked and reached Edinburgh at the end of May, 1850.

Second Visit Home, 1850-1855. Financially Dr Duff was sorely needed, though a week of collecting had removed a previous deficit of $27,500. Such sporadic efforts would not do. Duff had on shipboard evolved a scheme which he hurried to the Assembly to advocate. Though his five addresses did not secure his four points,—a day of humiliation and prayer for the Church's neglect of the heathen, regular weekly subscriptions for missions, a rule of proportion concerning the objects aided, and a synod in which to try the experiment,—he was granted a quarterly Association in every congregation to forward these objects. Sent forth by this "Foreign Missions Assembly," he went everywhere establishing associations for prayer, information and the quarterly collection of subscriptions. The result of this prolonged campaign, extending into all parts of Scotland and into England and even Wales,—where he spoke at one time to over fifteen thousand,—was the establishment of his far-reaching scheme in five hundred out of the then seven hundred of the Free Church congregations.

The distinguished honor of being Moderator of the Assembly of 1851 and his part in the *famous Educational Despatch of July, 1854*, are worthy of mention. The latter service was of incalculable value to India. Attending for hours each day sessions of the Committee with fellow-witnesses like John Stuart Mill and Prof H. H. Wilson, and cross-questioned on more than one occasion for five hours at a stretch, in the presence of persons like Macaulay, Disraeli and Gladstone, his educational and editorial experience gave his words weight. The result was that he and Mr Marshman worked out the educational part of the Despatch of 1854. His "handiwork can be traced not only in the definite orders, but in the very style of what has ever since been pronounced the great educational charter of the people of India." By it were secured Government inspectors, universities like that of London, secondary schools, improved primary and indigenous schools, grants-in-aid of all, degrees of the same for all in any institution who attain to a certain standard, normal schools, school-books, scholarships, public appointments, medical, engineering and arts, colleges, and also female schools. The grants-in-aid proposal, so fruitful in good, was urged by Duff "as the only just alternative, if the state persisted in refusing the Bible to be taught, under a conscience clause, in its colleges, as the Koran and the Vedas are taught."

In America, 1854. Interjected into this stay at home came an epoch-making three months in the States and in Canada. Brought here by Mr Stuart of Philadelphia, he was received in a terrific snow-storm by seventy ministers at eleven at night. This was a presage of the tremendous enthusiasm with which he was greeted from Boston to St Louis, and from Montreal to Washington. Whether preaching before Congress or talking to a Sunday-school class, he was everywhere the hero of the hour. *The impression left by his stay*,—during which he was the animating spirit of the first Union Missionary Convention held on this continent,—is thus described: "Dr Duff is obviously laboring under ill-health, and his voice, at no time very strong, occasionally subsides almost into a whisper. In addition to this drawback, he has none of the mere external graces of oratory. His eloquence is unstudied; his gesticulation uncouth, and, but for the intense feeling, the self-absorption out of which it manifestly springs, might even be considered grotesque. Yet he is fascinatingly eloquent. Though his words flowed out in an unbroken, unpausing torrent, every eye was riveted upon him, every ear was strained to catch the slightest sound. Indeed, while all that he said was impressive, both in matter and manner, many passages were really grand." As to the effect on our missionary spirit, he stands perhaps above even our own Judson and the saint of the New Hebrides, Dr Paton.

But such a nervous strain, amounting to a "living martyrdom," could not long continue, and he left America with an LL. D., money for a new college in Calcutta, and an order to go to the water cure of Great Malvern.

Third Term in India, 1856-1863. A winter spent in southern Europe, Syria and Palestine, a return to Edinburgh for a glorious September, and then the Duffs again leave for their field. Passing through central India, he arrived at Calcutta in February, when the mutterings of the storm which was to burst in 1857 were beginning to be heard. During the awful period of the Sepoy Mutiny he was the careful observer and chronicler, the man who stood unmoved in the most dangerous part of the city and who could say after the most critical night, "I have not enjoyed such a soft, sweet, refreshing sleep for some weeks past," and the preacher, who, when the danger was past, delivered by request a Thanksgiving Sermon,—one of the grandest oratorical efforts of his life.

Three events of special importance broke in upon the routine of his college work. One was the establishment of his *Caste Girls' Day School*, an institution of the greatest worth to the higher classes. A second was the part Duff played in the origin of the famous *Calcutta University*, established by the Government. The real headship of this institution lay in his fertile and wise brain, though he declined to become its Vice-Chancellor. A third matter was *his withdrawal*, after nearly a third of a century, to home service. Not even the cry "Come home to save the mission!" would have moved him, had not his old enemy, the dysentery, which a voyage to China did not remove, compelled his consent. Again Calcutta was stirred. Scholarships were established in his name; portraits and busts of him were secured for educational institutions; addresses from different classes of the community poured in upon him; and his countrymen raised a fund of $55,000, upon the interest of which he afterward lived. With the well-merited eulogies of Sir Henry Maine and Bishop Cotton to remind India of brilliant service ringing in his ears, this veteran sailed to the shores of Africa to begin at Lovedale his labors as Director of the Free Church Missions.

Closing Years, 1864-1878. A dream of Duff's had been a sort of Protestant Propaganda College in Scotland, and now with his other duties he attempted to realize it. The first step was a missionary professorship in the Free Church Institution,—he had years before gotten an American Seminary to establish one,—and when money was raised he was the only person worthy to occupy it. Unfortunately he did not live to see the establishment of his Missionary Institute nor Missionary Quarterly, though his lectureship is giving the world such books as Monier-Williams' "Buddhism."

Full of labors as professor of Evangelistic Theology, as Director of the Foreign Missions of his Church,—greatly to their enlargement—and as general missionary adviser to America and Britain, were the fourteen years preceding 1878. Then, on February twelfth, from his books which he loved so well,—Carlyle, De Quincey, Milton, Cowper, Hooker and the rest;—from his friends, who deemed his presence an inspiration; from his Kirk, of which he was a chief ornament; from bonnie Scotland, which he loved with an undying passion; from his Indian friends and old pupils, with whom he lived in spirit; from a world, one of whose most useful factors he had been,—God called him home and he was not.

His funeral brought together about the bier magistrates of various ranks, the four Universities and the Royal High School,—professors and students,—and, for the first time in history, the three Kirks and their Moderators, together with representatives of the English, American and Indian churches. Laid to rest by peer, citizen, missionary and minister, his life furnished the theme for half of the pulpits in Scotland on the following Sabbath. Well spoke a woman who saw his body lowered into the grave, "His coffin should be covered with palm branches;" for a Christian conqueror was this Alexander, and he could in very truth sing Paul's pæan of victory, "I have fought the good fight, I have finished the course, I have kept the faith: henceforth there is laid up for me the crown of righteousness, which the Lord, the righteous judge, shall give to me at that day."

SUGGESTED READINGS.

Catholic Presbyterian, Article Alexander Duff, Vol. III.,Pp. 215, ff.
Duff: Indian Rebellion; Its Causes and Results, (1858).
  Missionary Addresses, (1850), I., II., III.
  Missions, the Chief End of the Christian Church, (1839).
  New Era of the English Language and English Literature in India, (1835).

W. P. Duff: Memorials of Alexander Duff, D. D. Especially Pp. 32-70.

Encyclopædia of Missions, (1891), Article Alexander Duff.

Lal Behari Day: Recollections of Alexander Duff, D. D., LL. D., (1879), Chs. v., ix., x., xvi.

London Quarterly, Article Alexander Duff, Vol. LIV., Pp. 93, ff.

Proceedings of the Union Missionary Conference, Held in New York in May, 1854.

T. Smith: Alexander Duff, D. D., LL.D., (1883), Chs. iv-x.

Vermilye: The Life of Alexander Duff, (1890), Chs. vi-xvi.

G. Smith: The Life of Alexander Duff, D. D., LL. D., (1879). Agitating for Missions in Britain, Vol. I., Chs. x-xii.; Return to Calcutta, Vol. I., Ch. xiii.; Second Term in India, Vol. I., Ch.xiv. to Vol. II., Ch. xix.; Second Furlough in Britain and America, Vol. II., Chs. xx-xxii.; Last Term in India, Vol. II., Chs. xxiii, xxiv. · Final Years in Scotland, Vol, II., Chs. xxv-xxix.

THE MAN MACKENZIE, HIS FIELD AND PEOPLE.

It was not merely an enthusiasm for humanity that touched Mackenzie's heart and made him willing to give up his life for the benefit of the millions of China. Men have done noble deeds under the stimulus of philanthropy, but a higher motive than this was the mainspring of his life, and that was a consuming love for his Divine Master.—*Mrs M. F. Bryson.*

Early Days. In the isle so dear to England's late poet laureate and to her Queen, near its western end, lies the decayed town of Yarmouth. In that out of the way, fen-begirt place was born on the twenty-fifth of August, 1850, John Kenneth Mackenzie, destined in after years to prove one of the most important factors in the medical and missionary history of China. But he did not long remain in that land of downs and forests and picturesque watering-places; for in infancy his parents took him to the home of his boyhood and youth, the mercantile city of Bristol, seventy miles to the northwest of his native Isle of Wight. In this city, which had in 1497 sent forth John Cabot to discover in Nova Scotia the mainland of North America, and where in 1838 was built the first trans-Atlantic steamer, the boy Kenneth received those impulses which made him first a Christian, then an active worker for his Master, and finally a medical missionary.

The north of Scotland gave him a staunch Presbyterian father, while southern Wales furnished him with a beloved mother. His biographer is probably correct in saying that "to *his Highland blood* doubtless he owed a certain reticence of manner, combined with an intensity of feeling, which in a marked degree characterized his likes and dislikes." The *Welsh blood* in his veins may have aided him, as it usually does those of that nationality, in gaining a facile use of one of the most difficult tongues of the world, and it very probably had much to do with that love of preaching which colored his medical work.

His boyhood was passed in the helpful, Christian surroundings of a Presbyterian elder's home, so that religion was affecting him even before he was conscious of the fact. Not that he was a boy saint, however; for he had a hasty temper and was outspoken in defending any position which he might take, while as a pupil in Dr Stone's private school he disliked study, preferring the active sports of boyhood to irksome books.

At fifteen he left school and became *a clerk* in a merchant's office. He now began to appreciate the opportunities which he had hitherto partly wasted, and spent his spare hours in instructive reading. He also availed himself of the advantages of the Christian Association, which by its manifold activities has been so beneficial to many young men.

Beginnings of His Christian Life and Usefulness.
The unconscious workings of the Spirit in his early years became intensified on *two momentous days*, both of them times of special interest in the Association. The first of these was a certain May Sunday in 1867, when the topic of the Bible-class had been "A Good Conscience." It was an unusually impressive hour and at its close Mr Moody, then visiting England for the first time, made an address. Though he rose for prayers and dated his earnest desire for a spiritual life from that day, he was not one of the fifteen who then decided for Christ. Months of alternate struggle and discouragement followed until the anniversary of Mr Moody's address arrived. W. Hind Smith, the London Y. M. C. A. Secretary, delivered the address before the Association on that day, and at the solemn moment when he asked the young men to openly accept or reject Christ, the decisive hour for Mackenzie had struck, and from that time he was Christ's. On the way home, he and three companions stopped on a hill top, and like the Japanese youths of Kumamoto, dedicated themselves to be henceforth trustful, leal-hearted followers of their Master. Four

months later Kenneth united with the Presbyterian Church of Bristol and came under the moulding influence of that powerful preacher and earnest Christian, Rev Matthew Dickie, to whom he became greatly attached.

Young Mackenzie did not wait long before he engaged in *active work;* for he could not conceive of a true Christian who was not about his Father's business. First crucifying his pride by distributing tracts on a crowded thoroughfare, he later became leader of a band of workers who held open-air services, visited lodging-houses, taught in ragged schools and, as occasion offered, spoke at religious meetings and preached in outlying villages.

Mackenzie soon became conscious of his unfitness for these higher forms of work, and so we see him organizing a mutual *Christian training school.* In a broken-down cow-shed, two miles out of town, a little group of them would meet at five in the morning to read and criticise specially prepared sermons. His discourses were of great excellence, and this work, together with the ardent prayers poured forth as they knelt on the earth floor of the cow-house, enabled him to engage in the winter theater services. His ardent soul could rest in nothing but the most active service of the lowest, so that he is seen at one time winning a notorious king of thieves, at another bringing to the feet of Jesus attendants at the Midnight Mission.

Interest in Missions. The Christian workers with whom he came in contact were a source of rich blessing to him. One of these, Colonel Duncan, he felt a special love for, and to him he confided on his way home from a theater service a secret desire which had come into his heart, to engage in foreign missionary work. This wish had been begotten of the Spirit, through the *reading of biographies* of William Burns and Dr James Henderson, both laborers in China. Mr Duncan was very sympathetic but advised him, in view of his youth and limited education, to spend a number of years in a medical school in preparation for medical service abroad. Mrs Gordon's little book, "The Double Cure; or What is a Medical Mission?" was loaned him with the result that he felt that God would have him give up business and study medicine.

When he laid this proposition before his parents, he found them unwilling to consent to such a plan. Going to the Colonel with this *obstacle*, he proposed that young Mackenzie, John Gordon, whose wife had written "The Double Cure," a Bristol surgeon named Steele, and himself, should lay the matter before the Lord in prayer. This plan had scarcely become operative before his parents' objections disappeared. So at the very begining of his missionary career, he learned one of the secrets of his fruitful life, the power of prayer and the special value of united supplication for definite objects.

Preparation for Medical Service. Though without the basis of a college course, young Mackenzie had unusually good opportunities for securing a thorough medical training. For four years at the Bristol Medical School, and later taking special work in the Royal Opthalmic Hospital in London, he passed in Edinburgh his Licentiate of the Royal College of Physicians examinations, while at London he obtained the diploma of Member of the Royal College of Surgeons. During these years he had not intermitted his Christian work,—though naturally it was lessened in amount,—nor had his interest in missions decreased.

Appointment under the London Missionary Society. Before going to Edinburgh, Mackenzie had heard a stirring address from Rev Grffiith John, one of China's greatest missionaries. This only increased his interest in that field, and when at the Scotch capital, he interviewed Dr Lowe, of the Edinburgh Medical Missionary Society. Mr Bryson, Mr John's colleague, was eventually questioned and the need of Hankow seemed so great that he decided for China, though on the very day on which he offered himself to the L. M. S., he had two appointments brought before him for decision. With his early impatience and ignorance of the necessary routine of missionary organizations, he fretted because an immediate reply did not come from the Society. As soon as possible, however, he was gladly welcomed and appointment followed.

His conscientiousness caused him to lay every matter before the Lord, so that the date of his sailing and the question of marriage were both made matters of prayer. The

Society rather unwisely advised his starting in April—a step which they afterward regretted because of fever contracted in his first summer,—but he assented. Mr John's advice concerning the advisability of not marrying until after he had been in China for two years, that he might get well grounded in the language and in his medical work before the additional cares of a family came upon him, was also heeded.

Journey to China. Bidding his parents a sad adieu on April 8, 1875, he went up with his brother to London where he had time to attend once more Mr Moody's meetings. He had a few weeks before enjoyed a "never-to-be-forgotten" interview with the great evangelist, and all through his life he carried the memory of his evangelical zeal and activity.

Boarding the "Glenlyon," he left London, April tenth. His social nature soon gained him the friendship of sailors and passengers, with whom he was equally at home as quoit-player or preacher. Reading such books as Carlyle's "French Revolution" and Macintosh's "Leviticus" occupied his time, except that he meditated on the life before him with deep heart-searching. Thus he writes one Sunday: "I have had sweet communion with God this evening, and have enjoyed much comfort from the study of the Word to-day. I see that there are no two courses; it must be all for Christ, or else the soul gets dead and cold. Doing everything for His glory, and making His glory our object in every matter,—then only is there joy and peace. O Lord, may it be thus with me!"

Hong Kong was reached on May twenty-fifth, Shanghai on the third of June, and then after a river voyage of 600 miles up the Yang-tzu, he arrived on June eighth at his new home in Hankow.

Life in Hankow. China welcomes are peculiarly delightful, and in Mackenzie's case he was received into a very select circle, whose crown were Mr and Mrs Griffith John. As Bible translator, preacher, missionary champion and author of some of the most widely useful tracts in the language, Dr John was an incalculable aid to the young missionary. Mrs John, too, was indefatigable in her efforts to aid all, especially the sailors on the tea-steamers who are so numerous during the tea season. Into her work Mackenzie entered the first Sunday after his arrival, and during his three years in that city he was a large factor in a work which resulted in many conversions.

His first Monday saw him settled and beginning in earnest the *study of the language*, a process thus described: the teacher and I "sit down together with the same book. He calls over the words and I try to imitate him; my mouth is forced into all sorts of odd shapes, and I struggle on. The idea is first to get the proper sound, the meaning afterwards, and then—probably the most difficult—to learn the characters. We go on for about three hours, until I am tired of repeating sounds after him." This study was unfortunately interfered with by the pressure of medical work, as was the time for exercise, so that as the result of his own experience he writes to a young physician who came out years later: "If I were you I would not touch medicine for at least a year, but give your whole strength to the language and to looking after your own health. Medical missionaries are usually forced into medical work from the beginning, and then have to lament it ever after. Get a good foundation laid in the language, and take plenty of exercise in the open air." By utilizing spare moments, Mackenzie was able, after two years, to say that he enjoyed a Chinese sermon as much as one in English, and his biography tells of times when he could get a good look into the Classics and find joy in William Burns' incomparable version of the "Pilgrim's Progress." In the absence of larger opportunities for language study, he comforted himself in the significance of *his Chinese name*. This in Hankow was represented by three characters, Ma-kun-ge, *Ma* being his surname, the *kun* meaning "root" and the *ge* meaning "to relieve." It was his business, therefore, if true to his root, to relieve others' woes.

The *street chapel* was a place which the Doctor visited as often as possible, there to watch one of the most successful Chinese preachers do his work. The motley company of coolies, tradesmen and scholars to whom Mr John would try for two hours at a time to impart one great idea, gave him a valuable lesson and made him feel that ordinary discursive preaching was a sheer waste of time, and that no great results were to be expected unless one were willing to settle down to patient persevering work which the Spirit might use.

Mackenzie was wise enough to do what many missionaries neglect; he tells very vividly of visits to such places as the hall where the horrors of the Buddhist Hades are displayed in most gruesome fashion, and other matters connected with Chinese religion were also investigated.

An event occuring while at Hankow had its large influence upon Mackenzie's life. While engaged in Christian work at Bristol he became acquainted with Miss Millie Travers, a fellow worker, and later they were engaged. In 1876 he felt that the time had come for their union, and she accordingly came out to Shanghai, where they were married on the ninth of January, 1877. She was a true help-meet for him, and he greatly enjoyed his home and the joint work which they were now able to do. But her health was an uncertain quantity and in less than two years when their home had been brightened by the birth of their only child, Margaret Ethel, family complications and personal matters caused Mackenzie to ask to be sent to a new station in Ssu Chuan. The Society decided not to establish work at that place, but re-appointed him to Tientsin, the port of Peking in North China.

Transfer to North China. During these three years and a half Dr Mackenzie had won golden opinions for his art from all classes of the community and from the native Christians, who rarely see a physician so ready and anxious to help in the spiritual work of the mission. It was with pain, then, and in the midst of sorrowful adieus, that he left the city in March, 1879. The presence of Bp Schereschewsky and a consequential Salt Commissioner, relieved the tedium of the voyage, and when on the ocean they stopped a little at Chefoo, thus giving Mackenzie a glimpse of Dr Brereton's hospital. Thence to the bar off Taku, past its mud forts and into the sinuous Pei-Ho, seeming to him like a mill-stream meandering through fens, when compared with the majestic Yang-tzu, Son of the Ocean. The bund at Tientsin was reached on the twelfth and the party were most cordially received by members of the mission. His life here is in many ways a repetition of that at Hankow, save that it was far more momentous, as will be seen later.

Influences Affecting Mackenzie's Life. It may be well to note here some of those influences which had a developing effect on his life, for with him there was constant growth.

Men were his teachers very largely. Contact with earnest believers had a quickening influence upon him. The Cambridge Band stopped at Tientsin on their way to Shansi and their meetings and conversations gave him the greatest single impulse of his life, perhaps. A brief acquaintance with one of the most talented of England's young physicians, so early to yield his saintly life to Chinese service, Dr Schofield, was an experience of a life-time. So, too, was converse with the hero of Mongolia, a missionary Robinson Crusoe and evangelical exile, James Gilmour. One cannot help seeing in his after life the deep impress of these men and of Chinese Gordon, whose unique views he so fully expressed to Mackenzie.

Akin to these influences were those coming from *the printed page*. Bp Pattison, from the South Seas, inspired him; devotional writings of men like Murray were carefully digested and became part of his spiritual fibre; but above all other books, the Bible stood as the one preeminently loved. The writer well remembers his library with its rows of volumes, and the comparatively few which were well worn. One of his choice souvenirs is a set of old Bengel's "Gnomon," quaint and pithy, which Mackenzie had marked copiously. As his life ripened and spiritual discernment grew clearer, even Bengel and Murray were neglected in his absorbing love of the Word itself, so that at the end he was the man of one Book. How much he used this friend may be judged from the fact that a new copy of the Bible which had been his but three months, had been marked in every part, and in many portions carefully studied.

Providences were Mackenzie's teachers also. Nothing drove him to God so effectually as obstacles. No matter whether the difficulty was a critical operation, money for a hospital, particular kinds of cases which he preferred to have in his care, the hostility of natives inflamed to hatred by stories, or any other burden, his hour of weakness was "the wished, the trysted hour" when he was sure his Lord would fulfill his promises. The prayer-life thus engendered was one of the marked characteristics of the man. His Bible had prayer-slips in it; his letters are full of exhortations to prayer, or objects for which he wishes definite petitions offered. In one letter he proposes a plan for interesting little groups of Christians at home in particular Chinamen for whom prayers were needed, their interest to be sustained by frequent letters of information concerning them. The peculiar circumstances of his wife's health, which bereft him of her while she still lived, had a most hallowing influence over his remaining years.

It must be confessed that his last months saw the *growth of an ascetic element* which was not quite healthful. In his early years in China, he had been scrupulous about exercise, and after reaching Tientsin, he had attributed his excellent health to horse-back riding, as also to tennis, skating and walking, of which he was very fond. Toward the close of his life he withdrew more and more from society,—having tried in vain to exercise a Christian influence in that way,—and gave up games and riding. Yet he was not exactly morbid; he was rather eaten up by his zeal for his work and for his Saviour, from whom he could not bear to be long separated by even so thin a veil as that of the Christian's daily environment. Christian friends of deep spirituality had a growing value to him, and it was a pleasure to spend his time with them in Bible reading and prayer.

Relation to Others. To the people whom Mackenzie had left in England, he looked, in the earnest hope that they might be influenced to become helpers of the work abroad. When in 1883 he took his only furlough home, he was pained to see how little the children of God cared for their lost brethren and sisters in China; yet this did not prevent his being a useful speaker to home audiences, not only along missionary lines but also in the awakening or development of spiritual longings. His father's letters coming to him in China were much prized and aided him greatly.

Mackenzie never forgot his *obligations to foreigners* in China. The work for crews on tea-steamers at Hankow, and his temperance and evangelical efforts for the marines and sailors who wintered at Tientsin constituted part of his service and were very fruitful. In the latter city, Mackenzie was often aided by surgeons connected with gunboats or vessels, and for these some effort was made, though with little success. Fellow missionaries of every denomination were stimulated by his earnest prayers and by his strong hold on the Bible. A special quickening like that mentioned by Mrs Bryson in his Hankow life, and the yearly wave of blessing received at the Week of Prayer services at Tientsin or Peking, marked upward bounds into a broader and higher life.

But his students and patients were his especial burden. For them his heart yearned and day and night his thought was how he might be most influential in winning them for Christ. The life of a genuine Christian and the truths of inspired Scripture were the two things which he was anxious to bring into heart contact with them. Few men have been so happy in Bible class work as he. Deep interest in the truth and the living out of this truth were the points which he impressed, both of which were to be attained only through the help of the Spirit.

In God's providence Dr Mackenzie was thrown into intimate contact with the real, though not nominal, Emperor of China, the *Viceroy Li Hung Chang*. To this man he fearlessly testified of the truth which is in Jesus, though with the result that the oriental Bismarck regarded him highly for his works' sake, but esteemed him mad in matters of religion. Many other lesser servants in Caesar's household came under his influence, but without a single conversion; indeed, no high official in China can be a consistent Christian since his official duties must include idolatrous worship.

Sickness and Death. While still in his full vigor, his Master called him. On Monday, March 26, 1888, he was smitten down with a fever, which later threatened to become small-pox. Less than six days of patient suffering, of last farewells, especially pathetic in the case of his chief native assistant, formerly a student at Philips, Andover, and then on Easter morning, "very early," "when it was yet dark," he ascended from his couch of pain on Chih Li's cheerless plain to the Paradise of God. Tientsin, meaning the Heavenly Ford, had been to him but the inn of a traveler journeying to Jerusalem, but his passing that way had drawn multitudes to him. What wonder then that when this "most important man in Tientsin" died the last words marked in his Bible before his sickness were fulfilled in him, "And all Judah and the inhabitants of Jerusalem did him honor at his death."

Mackenzie's Field. Before passing to the consideration of the special work which made him great, a glance should be taken of his field. China, with its teeming millions is one of the most favorable places in the world for the medical missionary. Mackenzie's first home was almost in the geographical center of the Middle Kingdom; indeed, Hankow, with its sister cities of Wuchang and Hanyang, on the confluence of the Han and Yang-tzu, is known as the "Heart of the Empire." There at the center of its commerce and at the headquarters of anti-foreign influences which have been responsible for much of the rioting and outbreaks of recent years, Medicine stretched forth her beneficent hand to still hostility. Hankow, with its 750,000 inhabitants huddled together in the narrow lanes characteristic of central and southern China, swept often by floods, and the perpetual victim of epidemics of all sorts, needed him when he came, but with that rejection of the best so fatal to the Chinese, it was necessary for him to earn his laurels before he wore them. Threading its narrow alleys and burrows, he was every one's friend, even when deadly diseases threatened his own life. Nor did he confine his labors to the great city. Frequent tours in the country by boat or on foot on narrow dikes, made among people who more than once stoned and beat him, as well as lauded his virtues and feasted him, brought the healing hand and Christ-like voice, so attractive to simple-minded folk, into close contact with them.

When summer malaria or overwork drove him from his post for needed rest, he enjoyed greatly the mountain scenery of the lovely Lu-Shan, where a foreign bungalow sheltered him, or the quiet of the lakes, and especially the luxury of being at last in a place where he and his wife could walk about without the following of the elsewhere omnipresent, curious crowd of gaping on-lookers.

A less interesting country greeted him when he transferred his work to the northern end of that large plain of northeastern China whose fertile fields contain a population almost three times as great as that of the United States. In the winter season resembling an almost treeless expanse of clay colored soil, relieved by countless groups of grave mounds and frequent villages, this plain suddenly assumes a tropical aspect when the rains and fiery sun of summer cover it with heavy crops and abundant pools. In the winter Mackenzie would occasionally don his fur cap and warm Chinese foot-gear, and mounting the heavy springless cart of the north, run out into the villages and towns whence his patients had come. What cared he for the bedlam and vermin of inns and their brick beds, when he could reach grateful patients, who were only too glad to receive the Christain Tai-fu, Great-father? But in the north he had no beautiful Lu-Shan to which he could flee in time of sickness; instead, the mouth of the Pei-ho, with its mud flats and homes of pilots, was his place of refuge and furnished him with pure air and sea breezes as their only attractions.

His People. We shall see in the following chapter of what sort they were, medically considered. But as he met them day by day they at once attracted and repelled him. Their duplicity and honesty, conservatism and conservation of the best as they apprehend it, cruelty and tenderness, atheism and many gods, and a host of other qualities expressed by similar antonyms, were his constant study. His general estimate of them is thus recorded: "The more I know of the Chinese, especially of their educated men, the more I feel that there is a mine of wealth here. The leaven will take long to spread, but it is already at work. The inhabitants of the Pacific Islands are rapidly influenced in comparison with the Chinese, but though the process here will be slower, it will be far mightier in results."

SUGGESTED READINGS.

Burns: W. C. Burns, (1870).
Coltman: The Chinese, (1891), Chs. I-VII.
Douglas: Society in China, (1894), Chs. VI, VII.
Encyclopædia of Missions, (1891), articles J. Kenneth Mackenzie, and China, especially Pp. 255-264.
E. M.: The Chinese; Their mental and Moral Characteristics, (1877).
General Encyclopedias, articles Hankow and Tientsin.
Gordon: The Double Cure; or, What is a Medical Mission?
Henry: The Cross and the Dragon, (1885), Ch. III.
Holcomb: The Real Chinaman, (1894).
James Henderson, (1873).
Leisure Hour, Vol. XL., Pp. 777, ff.
Robson: Griffith John, (1889).
Smith: Chinese Characteristics, (1894).
Bryson: John Kenneth Mackenzie. Early Days, Ch I.; Student Life and Voyage to China, Ch. II.; Life in Hankow, Ch. III.; His Northern Home, Ch. VIII.; His Inner Life, Chs. XIV., XV.; Last Things, Ch. XVI.

MACKENZIE, THE MEDICAL MISSIONARY

A little while for winning souls to Jesus,
Ere we behold His beauty face to face;
A little while for healing soul diseases,
By telling others of a Saviour's grace.
—*Lines sent Mackenzie by Dr Schofield's widow.*

Chinese Views of Medicine. Dr Mackenzie labored in a land where medicine was studied quite widely and where men of education acted as physicians. In order to appreciate more fully the value of his work, we should glance, at least, at the conditions which surrounded him in his work.

Surgery, which in so many lands has become an art while medicine is still a phase of superstition, has never been developed in China. "Surgical operations are chiefly confined to removing a tooth, puncturing sores and tumors with needles, or trying to reduce dislocations and reunite fractures by pressure or bandaging. Sometimes they successfully execute more difficult cases, as the amputation of a finger, operation for a harelip, and insertion of false teeth. . . . Turning in of the eyelashes is a common ailment, and native practitioners attempt to cure it by everting the lid and fastening it in its place by two slips of bamboo tightly bound on, or by a pair of tweezers, until the loose fold on the edge sloughs off." From the sixth century B. C., the surgeon has placed great reliance upon acupuncture and the moxa.

Perhaps one reason why the Chinese have made so little progress in surgery is the fact that they have made no use of dissection and depend for *their knowledge of anatomy* upon a copper model of a man, pierced with numerous holes and inscribed in different places with the names of the pulses, and upon two other anatomical figures made in 1027 A. D. to illustrate the art of acupuncture.

Their theory of disease might seem to us unique, did we not remember more senseless theories prevalent among other uncultured nations, and the further facts that in Greece, "the mother-land of rational medicine," the "temple sleep" and its dreams were the basis of priestly prescription. Hippocrates, whose name stands first in ancient medicine, held tenaciously to the theoretical notions of the four elements,—hot, cold, wet and dry,— and to the Hippocratic humors. The hardly less famous Galen placed great confidence in the doctrine of critical days, which he believed to be influenced by the moon, and seems to have relied more on amulets than on medicine. According to Chinese authorities disease is due to a "disagreement of the *yin* and the *yang*, [the male and female principles of Chinese philosophy], the presence of bad humors, or the more powerful agency of evil spirits, and until these agencies are corrected medicines cannot exercise their full efficacy." It is also supposed to be due to the onset of the five elements, —water, fire, wood, metal, earth,—or to their wrong reaction.

Their *materia medica* presents a strange conglomeration of useful, useless and harmful ingredients. A list of 442 medicinal agents shows that 71 per cent. are vegetable, 18 per cent. animal and 11 per cent. mineral. If one were to peep into celestial gallipots he might find such surprises as snake-skins, scorpion stings, rhinoceros-horn shavings, moths, oyster-shells, human and silk-worm secretions, tiger bones, etc. These and their effective remedies are nicely accommodated to the particular one of the nine classes of diseases with which the patient is afflicted.

Native Practitioners. The Chinese Dr Rhubarb does not arrive at his dignities without effort. His *course of study* is not definite, though it includes the mastery of certain treatises of acknowledged weight, many of them described in Wylie's "Notes on Chinese Literature." The prospective doctor is also suppposed to have gotten hold of some manuscript medical works of a physician of repute and to have looked, at least, at the diagram which presents popular opinion concerning the inner economy of man, a diagram much resembling the cross-section of an egg enclosing a pine-cone and half a dozen angle worms. No *diploma* is needed, the practitioner being kept in check by one of the sections of the Government Code which exacts various penalties, even to the beheading of the physician, of him who causes the death of a patient by departing from established forms.

Diagnosis is considered the main point by the doctor. Coming to the patient in some state, he *sees the disease*, as the phrase for the operation is translated. "The right hand is placed upon a book to steady it and the doctor, with much gravity and a learned look, places his three fingers upon the pulsating vessel, pressing it alternately with each finger on the inner and outer side, and then making with three fingers a steady pressure for several minutes, not with watch in hand, to note the frequency of its beats, but with a thoughtful and calculating mind, to diagnose the disease and prognosticate its issue. The fingers being removed, the patient immediately stretches out the other hand, which is felt in the same manner." With few questions concerning his symptoms, the doctor proceeds to write out the numerous ingredients of a prescription which is pretty sure to contain decoctions measuring into the pints or quarts, besides powders, boluses, pills or electuaries. This done and the fee—"golden thanks"—received, he departs to return no more unless invited. As for the victim—who is literally a patient,—he may have resorted to the lot in order to learn what physician to employ. If so, the same man is asked to return again. In case he has bargained with a doctor to cure him in a certain time, he lays aside all work and ceases to eat that he may give his entire time to swallowing horse doses of all sorts of concoctions. If at the expiration of the time, he is not cured, a new physician is called in and eventually the patient dies or recovers.

Chinese Hospitals. Before the introduction of Christianity into the Empire, these were unknown, unless one considers foundling hospitals and lazarettoes as such. In the latter the poor leper can secure a fairly comfortable close to his wretched life by the payment of a sufficiently large fee. In the foundling hospitals the visitor chiefly remarks the dirt, the large mortality and the fact that the babies never cry, being constantly drugged.

Mackenzie's Two Hospitals. To such a medical need he had come to minister, but he was pained to find at the outset a deeply-seated prejudice against foreign medicine. The fact that foreign physicians ask questions of a patient instead of learning his condition from the light and heavy pressure on the inch, bar and cubit pulses of the two wrists, as well as the stories about foreigners' gouging out native eyes and hearts, with which to make medicines, telescope lenses and famous elixirs, had strengthened the ever-present conservatism into a virtual Chinese Wall which had first to be overthrown.

1. The Hankow Hospital. This was all ready to hand, having been cared for since 1866 by Drs Reid and Shearer. The building, erected at the joint expense of the foreign community, native merchants and the London Mission, is thus described by Mackenzie: "The hospital is a fine, substantially-built, roomy building, very well ventilated and arranged. On the ground floor at the back is the chapel, seating about 250 people; here there is preaching every morning to patients and to any others who may drop in from the streets. In front of the chapel is the dispensary and consulting room, where the patients are seen, a vestry for the missionaries, and a room in which the resident assistant lives. On the upper story are two large wards, two small ones, and a good-sized ward for foreigners; the naval surgeon sends his worst cases here. Outside the general building is a woman's ward and two other small buildings, used as schoolrooms, with the porter's lodge. Trees are planted all round the building, so that it has quite a pleasant appearance."

2. The Tientsin Hospital. When he arrived at this port the Mission had no hospital, though a medical work had been carried on since 1869, by a native dispenser, trained in Peking by Dr Dudgeon. Dr Mackenzie found this man without foreign drugs, and practicing much after the native fashion. Himself without money to buy medicines, he could only sit down and try to adjust his tongue to the new dialect, while he united with his colleagues in earnest prayer that God would open a door of escape from their financial dilemma. These prayers resulted in the determination to draw up *a petition to Viceroy Li*, "setting forth the advantages of establishing a hospital for the benefit of the Chinese, telling him what had been done elsewhere in medical missionary enterprise, and soliciting his aid." Although this memorial was written in perspicuous Chinese and presented by the very influential American, Mr W. N. Pethick, it received no attention.

Prayers, however, were doing their work. At the prayer-meeting of the Mission on the first of August, the topic was, "Ask, and it shall be given you," a promise which those present again pleaded in the matter of the memorial. As the meeting was breaking up, a courier from the Viceroy arrived with the request that Mackenzie would hasten with Dr Irwin to his residence, to attend his wife. That morning a member of the British Legation had been with the Viceroy, and noticing that he was sad, inquired the cause. When informed of *Lady Li's serious illness*, he suggested that foreign physicians be summoned. His excellency objected that it would be impermissible for her to be attended by a foreigner, but his good sense finally overcame immemorial custom, and the two physicians were called. Prayer was the more instant when so critical a case was undertaken, and God was pleased to use their efforts to the recovery of the illustrious patient. During convalescence Mackenzie suggested that Miss Dr Howard, then in Peking, be invited to remain at the lady's residence until she had entirely recovered. This resulted in the establishment by Lady Li of a woman's hospital, which was placed in Dr Howard's charge, and soon passed into the hands of the Woman's Society of the Methodist Board North.

While Mackenzie was still attending Lady Li, he and the community physician, Dr Irwin, gave *an exhibition of foreign surgery* in the presence of the Viceroy, which even more favorably impressed him. He had appointed these two men as physcians to his own family, and when the question of salary came up, Mackenzie asked that none be given him, but that instead the expense of his medical work be defrayed. At first a room outside the official office was set apart for medical purposes, but as this was found to impede public business, a quadrangle in one of the finest temples of the city was assigned him. Thither and to other yamens in the city he went on a handsome pony provided by the Viceroy, attended by a groom and a military official appointed to escort him. The temple was three miles from his house and proper religious work could not be done at such a distance; hence plans were made for a hospital building on the London Mission premises. Subscriptions, coming mainly from wealthy Chinese patients, enabled him to erect one of the finest hospitals in North China.

This building has been thus described: "It is erected in the best style of Chinese architecture, and has an extremely picturesque and attractive appearance. The front building, standing in its own courtyard, is ascended by broad stone steps, which lead from the covered gateway to a verandah, with massive wooden pillars running along its whole length. A hall divides it into two portions. On the right side and in front is a spacious dispensary, which, thanks to the liberality of the Viceroy, is wanting in nothing, rivaling any English dispensary in the abundance and variety of the drugs, appliances, etc.; behind this is a roomy drug store. On the left of the hall is a large waiting-room, with benches for the convenience of the patients, and used on Sundays and other days as a preaching hall. Behind, and to one side, is the Chinese reception-room always to be found in a native building. The rooms are very lofty, without ceilings, leaving exposed the huge painted beams, many times larger than foreigners deem necessary, but the pride of the Chinese builder.

"Running off in two parallel wings at the back are the surgery and wards, the latter able to accommodate thirty-six in-patients. The wards in the right wing, four in number, are small, intended each to receive only three patients. . . . The wards are all furnished with kangs instead of beds, as is the custom in North China. These kangs are built of bricks, with flues running underneath, so that in winter they can be heated; the bedding is spread upon a mat over the warm bricks." This building was opened in the presence of the Viceroy and representatives of different consulates, and the following Sabbath a thanksgiving service was held there, attended by members of the various Tientsin churches.

Mackenzie's Assistants. The plant having been secured, proper assistants were required. With so few Christians to select from, it became a matter for earnest prayer, just as had the erection of the hospital. When secured they needed to be trained, and all this work fell upon Mackenzie's shoulders.

As in every port, and especially where a river is ice-bound for three months each year, thus necessitating the stay in the city of surgeons of various gunboats, it was easy to secure *volunteer assistants*. Some of these men were extremely helpful medically, though as they did not know the language and were in many cases not Christians, they did little for the spiritual side of the work.

The First Government Medical School. A more competent company of assistants was needed than his dispensers constituted; hence when the Government recalled the students sent to America under Yüng Wing's Educational Commission, Mackenzie petitioned the Viceroy for eight of them, and with them the first Government Medical School began. While it was a joy to teach these bright fellows, and though Mackenzie was assisted by Dr Atterbury of Peking, the community physicians and the surgeons on duty at Tientsin and later by two medical colleagues, the brunt of the work fell on the Doctor himself. The eight proved apt students, and after completing a full course, they received buttons corresponding somewhat to those of civil officials of the Empire.

What to do with *the graduates* was then the problem. Receiving government appointments, they found themselves under the corrupt officials of army and navy, whose peculations drained off all the medical appropriations, thus leaving them only practitioners of the old sort to compete with on the basis of native medicines, which were cheap and so obtainable. This was a deep disappointment to them and to their instructor, and only a week before his death, when asked about his students, Mackenzie said that it was his intention to close the medical school soon. Happily this was not done, as that period was the darkness before dawn, and his successor was able to report a better state of things.

Statement of Cases. Dr Mackenzie's general practice presents the ordinary features of Chinese hospitals. *Outdoor patients*, as usual, were unsatisfactory, as medicines are often taken in doses many times greater than prescribed, proper care and diet are almost impossible, and the native custom of running to another physician, if relief is not immediate, militates against successful treatment. The commonest diseases thus treated were,—stated in descending order of frequency,—dyspepsia, chronic rheumatism, asthma, ringworm and bronchitis. *In-door patients* were in the wards about three weeks on an average, thus securing most favorable health conditions, and furnishing an admirable opportunity for religious impression and instruction. Diseases of the eye were most common, and then followed those of the digestive system, of the bones and joints, of the respiratory and the nervous systems. Of *operations*, the most common were those performed on the eye, after which came amputations, dislocations and fractures. This abstract hardly gives a fair account of the diseases of China; for, like Dr Parker, who in 1834 "opened China to the gospel at the point of his lancet," Mackenzie sometimes selected his patients, taking in those whom native practitioners could not aid, and rejecting those cases which were chronic or hopeless.

Opium work was made much of, though he hardly kept a refuge for these unfortunates. Out of an experience with nearly a thousand such patients, Mackenzie writes: "The habit of opium smoking, prolonged for any length of time, plays havoc with the man's natural energy, rendering him indolent and enervated. Few, in this condition, can, unaided, combat the craving for opium and effectually reform. The attempt is often made, but as often ends in disappointment. For a time they persevere, but when the intolerable craving, accompanied by extreme bodily depression, with violent achings of the joints and muscular pains, sets in, they fly to their old enemy, and drown themselves in opium stupor." Concerning the treatment, he says: "There is no medicinal specific guaranteed to cure; the object aimed at is to relieve symptoms as they arise, and so to help the patient back to health and freedom. I always tell them the medicine given them is to relieve the pain and craving, but they are to pray to God and believe in Jesus, to get the desire taken away from their hearts, and new hearts given to them."

Of course *unusual cases* were encountered, and he smiled many a time at medical incidents in native practice. Thus he notices a physician pretending to remove worms from teeth to cure toothache; another thrusts a needle many times into the gastric region to cure dyspepsia; a young fellow comes for treatment, from whose arm a piece has been cut out and administered to a sick father as an infallible remedy; a girl of six is seen, upon whose stomach is laid a large toad, while doses of scorpion-sting broth are given. On one occasion he was called to see a man who was laid out in his grave clothes, and whose daughter urged him not to delay his demise, as she was ready for his death. In still another case he is summoned to a man who had been some time in his coffin. He removes a tumor weighing twenty-five pounds; he gives sight to two girls blind from birth because of cataract, and as a result a church of more than a hundred members springs up; he amputates a girl's foot, leaving her a heel to walk on; he attends a Taoist priest who had his ears nailed for two days to his temple door to raise funds for its repair; he inserts a silver tube in a man's windpipe, with the result that he gained the reputation of giving men two mouths.

The Question of Fees. Mackenzie felt strongly on this matter. From the poor he did not wish to receive anything, and in general, to avoid the imputation that his work was a mere matter of business, he refused remuneration. But he made it very clear to well-to-do patients that they owed a debt of gratitude for healing received, and from such he received enough so that he laid by for the hospital a reserve fund of over $10,000.

Spiritual Element in Mackenzie's Work. His one aim in coming to China was "to make medicine the handmaid of the gospel, seeking, through the administration of medical relief, to advance the cause of our Lord and Master Jesus Christ, thus combining the healing of the body with the curing of the soul, in accordance with the words of Scripture, 'And He sent them to preach the Kingdom of God, and to heal the Sick.'" We saw in the previous chapter that Mackenzie was a believer in Chaucer's doctrine that the teacher of Christ's lore and that of his apostles must first follow it himself. Looking to other lines of effort, we find the following especially emphasized.

1. He considered *prayer an essential part of his strength*. Opium patients and others, as has been stated, were bidden to pray for their double healing, while the Doctor himself never attempted an important operation without special prayer for the needed skill. He believed that every medical missionary should be a faith healer in this sense: "He should give all the attention possible to his case, use every means he can think of, every agency or drug that he knows of; but he should also do so in humble dependence upon God for His blessing."

2. *Preaching* was not merely *a* part of his work; it was one of the most important items in the day's program. He usually did some of it himself using such passages as the prodigal son, the barren fig tree, blind Bartimeus and the palsied borne of four, as his texts. During the entire time that patients were in the waiting room, someone was either talking or preaching to them.

3. But such formal work was less profitable than *conversational and instructional work* with individuals and little groups. One looking in upon the wards any afternoon might see knots of patients gathered about one or two beds listening to one of the hospital helpers as he spoke of the love of Jesus or tried to teach them the elements of Christian truth. He writes: "Portions of gospels and tracts are scattered about the wards, and as we pass from patient to patient, dressing wounds and attending to the wants of all, we question them upon the books by their side and exhort them to think of the truths of Christianity,

and thus have innumerable opportunities for individual dealing."

4. To prepare assistants for such work, Mackenzie emphasized *the Bible class*. The work was very interesting because made as conversational as possible. One class was held daily, except Sunday, for three quarters of an hour in the morning; another, on Tuesday evening, was used to gather up the work of the week and for drawing the net; a third on Friday evening was for helpers and Christians only; and still another was held on Sunday, when often people from the missionary ranks would drop in to enjoy his teaching. Much prayer accompanied these exercises and in addition the medical students were encouraged to hold private meetings by themselves.

5. The Doctor tried, also, to keep hold of patients who had become impressed with the truth, but who had gone to *distant homes*. At one time, he employed a special helper to visit such cases; at another, he himself went out touring to find such men, though the fear of neighbors that he had come to collect money from former patients, sometimes made the process of locating them difficult. Usually he was received most warmly by those who regarded him as their physical saviour, and as their dearest friend.

6. The *propagation of this evangelical crusade* constituted one of Mackenzie's important duties. In 1886 the Medical Missionary Association of China was established, as also its organ, "The Medical Missionary Journal." Mackenzie's work had been so intensely evangelical, that it became perfectly natural to ask him to edit its evangelistic department, and during the last fifteen months of his life, he contributed often to its pages. In one of these articles, "The Evangelistic Side of a Medical Mission," he urges every medical missionary to *engage personally in such work* for these five reasons: he can best influence his own patients; his assistants will be, under God, largely what he makes them; unless he attends to it, the full value of the medical mission as a Chistianizing agency will not be developed; his own spiritual life requires it; and it enables the physician to soar above the daily drudgery and the depressing influences of continuous labor among dirty and

sin-saturated wretches who throng missionary hospitals and dispensaries.

Tsung erh Yen Chih. This phrase, so often used by Mackenzie, and meaning a concise summary of what has been said or written, is not in his case exhausted when we say of him that he was a man placed in a providential relation to Li Hung Chang, who largely through his agency adopted modern medicine for army and navy, thus giving it entrance into the family of the Emperor himself, and favorably impressing many officials of high rank with the fruits of Christianity. Another man in his position might, perhaps, have done as much as he in such a direction. His service to the great cause which he represents lies in the magnificent object lesson of his godly life, and in the bright and cheerful Christianity which he represented to his medical students and to the medical missionaries of China, who knew him only to admire and emulate his spiritual qualities.

He has given us *the gist of that successful life* in these words: "One of the best ways in which the medical missionary can influence his patients is by keeping up the spiritual life of his assistants, encouraging them to prayer and the frequent study of the Scriptures. Of course, he can only aid them as he is himself abiding in Christ, and drawing strength and life from his Saviour. He cannot give what he has not himself got. The knowledge of this should stimulate us to a constant and close walk with God. It is of little account for us to pray for the outpouring of the Holy Spirit upon our assistants or patients until the great cry of our hearts is, 'Lord, fill me!' and then when we are full, from us will go forth streams of living water to those around."

SUGGESTED READINGS.

Century Illustrated Magazine, August 1896, Pages 560-571.
China Mission Hand-Book, (1896), Medical Statistics.
Coltman: The Chinese, (1891), Chs, VIII-X.
Creegan and Goodnow: Great Missionaries of the Church, (1895), Ch. x.

Doolittle: Social Life of the Chinese, (1865), Vol. I., Ch. v.
Douglas: Society in China, (1894), Ch. VIII.
Dowkount: Murdered Millions, (1894).
Dudgeon: The Diseases of China, (1877).
Encyclopædia of Missions,(1891), Article Medical Missions.
Foster: Christian Progress in China,(1889), Pp. 162-188.
Hanbury: Science Papers. (1876), Pp. 211-277.
Henry: The Cross and the Dragon, (1885), Ch. XIV.
Lockhart: The Medical Missionary in China, (1861), Chs. VI-X.
Lowe: Medical Missions, (1887), Ch. V.
Mabie: In brightest Asia, (1891), Pp. 91-95.
Missionary Review of the World,September, 1896, Pp. 664-680, 697.
Smith: Chinese Characteristics, (1894), Chs. XI., XVI.
Smith: Contributions to Chinese Materia Medica, (1871).
Stevens and Markwick: The Life of Peter Parker, M. D., (1896), Chs. VIII., IX.
Tenney: The Triumphs of the Cross, (1895), Pp. 613-617.
Williams: The Middle Kingdom (1882), Vol. II., Pp. 118-134.
Bryson: Johh Kenneth Mackenzie. Country Work and Persecution, Ch. IV.; Overcomimg Prejudice, Chs. VI., VII.; Medicine and the Viceroy, Ch. IX.; Chinese Medical Students, Ch. XI.; XII.; Strange Phases of Chinese Life, Ch. XIII.; Medical Review of Mackenzie's Werk. Appendix II.; Spiritual Side of His Work, Appendixes III., IV.

VII

MACKAY'S EARLY LIFE AND HIS AFRICAN FIELD

> His beauty and extraordinary gentleness, together with his wonderful aptitude for picking up all kinds of handicraft, speedily ingratiated him with the workmen, . . . When he appeared on the scene he was accosted with the question, "Weel, laddie gaen to gie's a sermon the day?" and the invariable reply (in which there was something like prophetic instinct) was, "Please give me trowel; can preach and build same time."—*Anecdote of Mackay at three years.*

Birth. Alexander Murdoch Mackay's sister, Mrs Harrison, vividly describes that snowy 15th of October, 1849, when one of Africa's greatest benefactors first saw the light. His father,—geographer, geologist and author, as well as Free Church minister,—is surrounded in his study by gazetteers, atlases, and books of travel, while on a nail hangs a map of Africa, and from the walls Disruption worthies and stern reformers look down. The infant Alexander, brought in by his nurse Annie, is unnoticed until she has listened to a geographico-missionary discourse on central Africa. This story is an essentially true one and ends with a prophecy when the father says: "The gospel banner will yet be planted at the very heart of this continent, although not likely in your day nor mine, Annie;" to which the good nurse replied, "But may be it'll be in your son's, sir! and wha will say he'll nae hae a han' in it?"

Birthplace. Alexander spent his early years in the highlands of Scotland at the little village of Rhynie, located inland in Aberdeenshire. Surrounded by the scenery of the Grampians and living at the foot of picturesque Tap o' Noth, the child could not but be responsive to influences which have helped make pure, strong and efficient many of his countrymen. Rhynie is a pastoral and sparsely settled district whose inhabitants, of Pictish origin, have always been strongly wedded to religion. Iron was in their blood, simplicity marked their lives, and independence their thoughts. The Bible was their household book and God their supreme and daily ruler. These Bible loving neighbors, his pious nurse, the heathery slopes of Noth, rippling burns running through the peat moss, whirring moor-cocks, bleating sheep and modest flowers constituted his early and helpful environment.

Parentage. Far more vital in their influence upon him than these surroundings were his parents. *Alexander Mackay* was to his son what James Mill was to John Stuart, though happily religion was not lacking either in Mr Mackay's life or in his conversation. An ardent student and a born teacher, he found time in his secluded parish to prepare various scientific books, but it was a greater delight still to instruct his boy who until fourteen knew no other teacher. He was a conservative educator, believing that mathematics and the classics were the best foundation for a general education. He had the rare faculty of making instruction interesting and rote-learning had to give place to clear reasoning. Alexander responded to such an instructor with a craving for knowledge which found its keenest satisfaction in long walks which were voyages of discovery in the world of nature. Other studies were also included in this peripatetic school, and the two often occasioned wonder as they paused while the father demonstraed in the sand by the roadside a geometrical proposition, or traced the probable course of the Zambesi. Minute observation and thoroughness were so enforced by this teacher that Mackay might have echoed John Stuart Mill's boast, "Mine was not an education of cram." Nor was it confined to material and speculative matters; for the cottage prayer-meetings and "catechising," where the Scriptures and Shorter Catechism were explained, gave the boy deep insight into the thoughts of godly men and of God himself.

If the father was Mackay's teacher, *his mother*, Margaret Lillie, of Huguenot descent, was the moulder of his character. She possessed much literary and linguistic ability,

—extending even to the Hebrew,—and so was an additional aid to Alexander, who not only acquired her style, but at the same time drank in tales of Disruption and Seceding heroes with the same eagerness accorded to stories of Huguenot martyrs. These recitals were usually followed by the injunction,

> "O ye who boast
> In your free veins the blood of sires like these,
> Lose not their lineaments."

Mrs Mackay made Sunday the happiest day of the week. After the Bible and catechism lessons were successfully mastered came the reward, "a missionary story," which she told most interestingly. In her childhood she had been deeply moved by a missionary sermon and the account of that experience gave Mackay *one of his first missionary impulses*. Mrs Mackay's life was saturated with Scripture and Alexander imbibed it most eagerly; though not until her death in his sixteenth year, when she left him her Bagster's Bible with the dying message to "'Search the Scriptures,' not to read them only, but to *search*, and then he would meet her again in glory," did he make them the guide of his life.

Boyhood. The influences already named produced their natural fruitage. *Intellectually* he was precocious. He read the New Testament fluently at three; at seven, "Paradise Lost," Russell's "History of Modern Europe," Gibbon's "Decline and Fall of the Roman Empire," and Robertson's "History of the Discovery of America" were his text-books, after which his reading lesson was the leading article in the newspaper fully explained by his father. Euler's Algebra falls into his hands when he is eight and opens up a fairy world to him. D'Aubigne's "Reformation," and indeed every other work that he found were fairly devoured.

In practical things, also, he was an eager learner. At three he imitates stone masons; at four when told to bring a heavy bar, he carries it by lifting it one end at a time and going around it. At nine years he feels that he is old enough to have a printing press, because Luther has said that "Printing is the latest and greatest gift by which God enables us to advance the things of the Gospel;" to which the boy added: "Skill takes no room in the pocket, . . . and some day I might find it useful." The press was bought and years afterward did " advance the things of the Gospel" on the shores of Victoria Nyanza. From eleven to thirteen years of age books were thrown aside and the garden and farm, the pony, locomotive engines, machinery and handicrafts of every description, occupied his thoughts. Though at fourteen he took up his books again at the Aberdeen Grammar school, even there the art of photography and the ship-building yard had a perfect fascination for him.

His *spiritual life* was always deepening, thanks to his mother's care. A strong sense of rectitude, dating from his fifth year and the Brig o'Bogie where nurse Annie threw the leather "tawse" into the water, Sunday teachings, parish catechisings, "Pilgrim's Progress' and Mrs Mackay's prayers were used by the Spirit to draw him to God.

All the while that *broader touch of the world*, so often denied country children, came to him. The best literature and periodicals, which he was required to read, made him a cosmopolitan, and his father's fame brought to the manse men like Hugh Miller and Sirs Roderick Murchison and A. Ramsay, who were greatly attracted by the boys' skill in map-drawing and type-setting. Men and women of the Drumtochty type also had a hardly less marked influence on him, provincial though they were.

Life In Edinburgh. Mr Mackay desired his son to be a minister, and the mother would gladly have seen him a missionary, but to neither of these was he inclined. Machinery and engineering were his deepest love, and when his father's financial limitations were a barrier to his entering on these studies, he went to Edinburgh and taught three hours a day to meet his expenses while studying. Two years, spent in the *Free Church Training College for Teachers*,—where he was marked ninety per cent. on the Bible, Geography, History, Arithmetic, Algebra, Geometry, Latin, Greek, School Management, Skill in Teaching and Theory of Music, and where he won prizes for drawing,—were referred to in Africa as being of great benefit. The next four years were busy ones. Engineering and kindred sciences were studied *at the University* for three years and one year was devoted to Surveying and Fortification. Meanwhile, besides his teaching and attendance on evening lectures, he spent the afternoons at Leith engaged in practical engineering.

Sundays were days of equal activity. At the church of Dr Horatius Bonar, who fostered in him "habits of reverent and constant fellowship with God, and daily study of the Holy Scriptures," he gained weekly strength. The afternoons found him conducting childrens' meetings or in mission halls, and in the evening he was a regular teacher at the Sunday-school connected with Dr Guthrie's Original Ragged School.

In Germany, 1873-1876. November 1st saw him *en route* for Berlin whither he went to master the German language as the key to its valuable lore, to perfect himself as an engineer and, above all, to "use every opportunity of diffusing scriptural truth and of winning souls for Christ." He readily secured a good position as draftsman on locomotives and portable steam engines in a large engineering firm, and found his fascinating employment tempting him to forget God. His fellow draftsman, moreover, were infidels and blasphemers, but he made this an occasion for doing personal work among them, for which he seeks McCheyne's equipment: "Some believers are a garden that has fruit trees, and so are usful; but we ought also to have spices, and so be attractive." Soon promotion came and he was made head of the locomotive department, with a larger sphere of influence.

Mackay's *religious life and usefulness* were greatly deepened and enlarged by notes of Dr Bonar's sermons, sent weekly by his sister, and especially by the friendship of Court Preacher Baur, who was drawn to the young Scotchman and invited him to live at his own home as his "dear son." Not only did this give him exceptional opportunities for learning German, but it also brought him into contact with the highest Christian society of Berlin, including the sister of Prince Bismarck. At the Bible readings given at Dr Baur's and through the Bible Class held on Sunday evenings he secured and imparted much good, especially in connection with American students. Other activities, such as personally inviting men to church and distributing tracts to cabmen, filled his leisure hours. What his life was religiously is described by a *journal kept at this period*, the pages of which are filled with sentences like these: "O for nearness to God! God grant me I pray Thee, a deep spirit of humility—the broken will and the contrite heart." . . "Slept in again. No time for prayer or reading God's Word in the morning. Yet the Lord is gracious to me." . . "Attaining day by day to a little more childlike faith in Jesus, and therefore joy and peace." . . "Teach me, my Saviour, to speak to lost souls in love." . . "Lord, bless abundantly two or three grains of seed sown. What an idle day!" . . "Since I came to Berlin I have been enabled to study much of the Word of God, and to find something of the inexhaustable mine of pure gold it contains. If I had been at home, surrounded by so many sacred influences, the probability is I might not have made so much progress. One thing above everything, I must make my Christianity a practical thing. 'It is more blessed to give than to receive.'"

The Missionary Call. Within six weeks after reaching Germany this call came to young Mackay. For some years he had not read nor thought much on missions, as his professional studies had crowded the subject into the background. In December an address on Madagascar by Dr Burns Thomson came into his hands, and this appeal, together with his mother's early injunction, "If the call comes to you, take care that you do not neglect it," and Dr Baur's deep interest in missions, so fired him with missionary zeal that he called it "a new conversion."

Other considerations also entered in. The texts coupled by his mother in his boyhood, "If ye love me, keep my commandments," and, "Go ye, therefore, and teach all nations;" her quotation of Dr Duff's words, "The advancement of the missionary cause is not only our duty and responsibility, but it is an enjoyment which those who have once tasted would not exchange for all the treasures of the Indian mines, for all the laurels of civic success, and for all the glittering splendor of coronets. It is a joy rich as heaven, pure as the Godhead, lasting as Eternity;" the old map of Africa, with the Mountains of the Moon lying like a huge caterpillar across his future field; the "Nile problem" which he and his father discussed so frequently; his puzzling over the reason why the Church Missionary Society should secure its agents in Germany instead of in England; the charm of "Livingstone's Travels;" his Christmas letter of 1866, in which he says, "I shrink from the ministry. . . . Besides it seems to me there are already too many ministers. Three or four wasting their energies in each little parish of Scotland may satisfy a desire for sermon hearing, but is attended, I fear, with little good;" the elaborate trivialities of modern life because of which an able writer says, "His brave and active nature would have beaten itself to death against the bars of European conventionality;" above all, his sister's letter of December 11, 1873, accompanying Dr Thomson's address:—all these were successive missionary impulses, culminating in what he deemed the voice of God calling him to Madagascar.

To be called meant immediate action to Mackay. The select Christian circle in which he moved were informed of his intentions, and Dr Baur encouraged him to be an engineering missionary. Licentious, drunken and infidel Berlin was a training school preparing him to combat idolatry. The study of Malagasy was enthusiastically, if unwisely, prosecuted. He sees clearly that "if Christianity is worth anything it is worth everything," and that he will be fit to win souls only so far as he attains deep spirituality and abiding fellowship with his risen Saviour. In 1875 a tempting professional offer came to him, which he declined as one article of his creed ran : " It is not to make money that I believe a Christian should live." He accepted, however, an engagement at Kottbus, sixty miles southeast of Berlin, and there employed his spare hours in sending to all the clergy of the Empire the German version of Bonar's "Words to Soul Winners," and also arranged for the translation at his own expense of "Grace and Truth."

Correspondence with Missionary Societies and Appointment. As Mackay's interest had been aroused through Madagascar, he wrote first to Dr Bonar and sought a position under *the London Missionary Society* on that island. Dr Bonar thought mission work and engineering difficult ideas to combine, and Secretary Mullens wrote, "that at that time the island was not ripe for his assistance." Mackay was not daunted, for he had "one word against such a problem, ' Jehovah Jireh!'" What he wished was an opportunity to wed civilization and Christianity in Africa, to execute works such as railways and mines, largely through natives trained in religion and science; in a word, he wished to supplement the work of other missionaries, not to supplant it. This desire was ultimately satisfied; for on a bitterly cold night in December, 1875, after finishing "How I Found Livingstone," his eye fell on an old copy of the Edinburgh Daily Review" in which *the Church Missionary Society* appealed for pioneers to go into Uganda in response to King Mtesa's invitation sent home by Stanley. Though after midnight, Mackay immediately wrote to the Society offering his services. Having heard of this correspondence, *Dr Duff urged him to wait* for an opening in the African missions of the Free Church of Scotland, or else to join the Established Church of Scotland's Mission on Lake Nyassa. But it was too late, for in the same mail came a letter from the C. M. S. Secretary accepting him as their missionary to Uganda, with the understanding that he was to combine industrial work with religious teaching. And so he turned from the church of his fathers to the Established Church of England and its society, the greatest Protestant missionary organization of the world.

Preparation for Sailing. As Mackay was to sail in April, the succeeding weeks were filled to the brim with preparations. Captain Grant, Speke's companion in Equatorial Africa, whose birthplace was scarcely fifty miles from Rhynie, gave invaluable advice, and grandly seconded by the C. M. S., this youngest member of the pioneer party of eight provided for his own and their needs. A boat for the Victoria Nyanza had to be secured with an engine of his own designing, the boiler of which was made of welded rings. He must learn more of practical astronomy and the use of the sextant; printing offices and photographers must be visited for last lessons; vaccination and the use of the stethoscope were yet to be learned, as also the details of iron-puddling and coal-mining. During these weeks "there was no such word as holiday in his vocabulary; his mission was to him a whole-souled passion and every hour was turned to practical account in picking up useful arts" Believing it not at all likely that eight Englishmen starting for Africa would all be alive at the end of six months and that "one of us—it may be I—will surely fall before that," but assured that "it is His cause—it must prosper, whether I be spared to see its consumation or not," he stepped aboard the steamship "Peshawur" on April, 27, 1876, and bade a last adieu to England.

En Route to Uganda. An uneventful voyage of seven thousand miles brought him on May 30th to Zanzibar, and soon thereafter on the main land his African career began. More than two years elapsed before he reached the shores of his inland sea, during which *the kaleidoscope of his life* exhibits him in all sorts of combinations. He is first explorer of the rivers Wami and Kingani; then caravan leader, slave exterminator, dying man, road maker, bridge builder, blacksmith, physician, ox driver, and preacher on Sunday when all tools were dropped. Now he is wading chest deep in a swamp: again he is burrowing through the dense reed tunnels of hippo and rhinoceros trails, and a third time while waiting for a rope with which to lasso a stump on the opposite side of a swift stream and so make a bridge, we see him taking a copy of "Nature" out of his pocket in order to master "Haeckel's Theory of Pangenesis, or the undulatory theory of molecules in organic life." In salt and waterless deserts, in unhealthful mangrove forests, on salubrious highlands, he thirsts and feasts and starves, sleeping nights, after he has written up his journal, in tents, hen-houses, huts whose floors are mire, cow pens and in the open air among zebras, giraffes, leopards, lions, elephants and more troublesome pests, such as gnats, mosquitos, scorpions, and ants of every variety. Decamping carriers, avaricious leviers of tribute with whom one must sometimes haggle for days, insolent chiefs, who for the luxury of lighting a parlor match exact a fine of twenty-five cloths, frequent thefts, a vast family speaking a babel of tongues none of which Mackay fully understood but whose mouths must be daily filled, even in the wilderness, chiefs with whom he entered into brotherhood and children who loved him,—these were his companions and this the pioneer who opened up a road 230 miles in length toward Victoria Nyanza.

When on June 13, 1878, he could shout his Thalassa! *on the southern shores of the lake* he was by no means home. His fellow missionaries, Lieut Smith and O'Neil, had been murdered on the island of Ukerewe and no one dared go with him to treat with their murderer. He accordingly went alone and returned only after the African bond of blood brotherhood had been cemented. Then kosmos must be made out of the chaos found in Kaduma's huge hut where the valuable property of the expedition had been piled together in hopeless confusion,—a ten days' task. The Daisy must be patched and later remade, and gimbals turned, on which Mackay's pocket compass may move, before he can set sail on a lake as large as Scotland. This sea of storms wrecked their little craft within a week. Two months passed before they could get away again, and it was not until November 6th that he finally reached his appointed field.

Uganda.* Stanley, whose challenge to Christendom led to the formation of the mission, called this most influential native kingdom, "The Pearl of Africa," a name which it deserves, as it also does that given it by the Arabs, "The Land of the Grave." Lying along the northwest shores of the greatest inland sea of the world next to Lake Superior, it covers with its dependencies a territory as large as Missouri, or as New England with an additional Connecticut. While it lies under the equator, its altitude,—4000 feet and upward above the sea level,—and frequent rains

---

*The natives call their country Bu-Ganda, U-Ganda being its name in Suahili, the language of the coast region. Similarly they call themselves Ba-Ganda (singular Mu-Ganda), and their language Lu-Ganda, while in Suahili the people are known as Wa-Ganda and their speech as Ki-Ganda. As the early missionaries learned Suahili first and as it was understood at the capital, these terms are often used indiscriminately.

make the climate cool, the annual temperature ranging from 50° to 90° F., though it rarely rises above 80° and seldom sinks below 60° at night.

The country is described as being in some parts a plain, but mainly a succession of hills, between which lie unwholesome swamps through whose masses of reeds and papyrus slimy streams slowly straggle. Some of the hills have a tropical appearance, due to the banana plantations. Most of them, however, are covered by a tangle of elephant grass fifteen feet high, impenetrable save by mice and elephants. These jungles harbor enormous pythons and innumerable wild beasts, of which the natives most fear the plantation-eating buffalo, and are vocal with the terrible plague of mosquitos. One standing on a hill top at sunset forgets, however, every disagreeable feature and is overpowered by the glory and transcendent delicacy of color on cloud and hill and lake.

The soil is fertile and produces indigenously plantains, cotton, coffee and tobacco. It is also friendly to sweet potatoes, beans, tomatoes, rice and Indian corn. The last, which has been the principal cereal, yields from three hundred to five hundred fold. The best time for sowing is at the period of the equinoctial rains, yet as it showers nearly every night, one can sow and reap on any day of the year. Below the surface lie iron in abundance and inexhaustible deposits of china clay. When the soil is turned up its decaying vegetation causes malaria, which disease is ever present, though not so deadly as the scourge of smallpox and the plague.

Early Visitors to Uganda. Speke and Grant were the first Europeans to reach this land. The former resided at the capital from February to July in 1862 and suggested it as a possible field for missionary effort. An officer of Col Gordon's again reached Uganda in 1874, but it was H. M. Stanley's visit in 1875 that was most memorable. King Mtesa received him hospitably, while Stanley, filled with the spirit caught from Livingstone, set before the King the claims of Christianity, and had written for him in Arabic the Ten Commandments, the Lord's Prayer, the Golden Rule and "Thou Shalt Love Thy Neighbor as Thyself."

Mtesa showed his interest by observing the Christian as well as the Mohammedan Sabbath and urged the explorer to secure Christian teachers for his people.

In response to this monarch's request, we see standing before him in November, 1878, a Scotchman in his thirtieth year, whom Stanley, eleven years later, *described* as a "gentleman of small stature with a rich brown beard and brown hair, dressed in white linen and a gray Tyrolese hat," . . "with calm blue eyes that never winked,"—"the best missionary since Livingstone."

SUGGESTED READINGS.

Colville: The Land of the Nile Springs, (1895), Ch. IV.

Creegan and Goodnow: Great Missionaries of the Church, (1895), Ch. XVII.

Drummond: Tropical Africa, (1888), Ch. III.

Encyclopædia of Missions, (1891), Articles Africa, Church Missionary Society, and Alexander M. Mackay.

General Encyclopædias, Article Uganda.

Harrison: Story of the Life of Mackay of Uganda, (1891), Chs. I-IV.

Larned: History for Ready Reference, (1895), Vol. V., Article Uganda.

Portal and Rodd: The British Mission to Uganda in 1893, (1894), Pt. I., Ch. VIII.

Stanley: Through the Dark Continent, (1878), Vol. I., Chs. IX., XII., XVI.

Harrison: Mackay of Uganda, (1890). Boyhood, Ch. I.; Life in Edinburgh and Berlin, Ch. II.; On the Road, Ch. III.; Arrives in Uganda, Ch. IV.

VIII

MACKAY'S PARISHIONERS AND HIS WORK

He was one of those few who look fearlessly forth and seem to see the face of the living God. He never despaired of any person or any thing. Quiet he was, and strong and patient, and resolute, and brave; one on whom you might depend. He endured fourteen years of Africa, . . . fourteen years of contradiction of men, black and white, fourteen years of dangers, fevers, sorrows, disappointment—and in all and through all he was steadfast, unmovable; a true missionary, always abounding in the work of the Lord."
—*Rev R. P. Ashe*, "Two Kings of Uganda."

The Baganda. Looking out from the temporary premises which had been occupied by Mr Wilson, Mackay's fellow-laborer and his predecessor by sixteen months at the capital, one could see on the hill-side well tilled gardens surrounded by tall tiger-grass fences and containing the beehive-shaped grass or straw huts of the Baganda. *These houses are described* as having doors facing the ascent, with clay ridges to prevent the flood of water from running into them. Their roofs are double, so that there is a good circulation of air. "The sleeping place is curtained off with bark cloth, and bedsteads are used, consisting of a framework of branches, which rests on stakes driven into the ground, and which is covered with fine grass and a mat. A large piece of bark cloth forms the coverlet. A square is marked off by four logs in the middle of the house for a fireplace, and the cooking-pot rests on three stones." Here are prepared the two meals of each day, consisting of bananas or plantains, beef, goat's flesh or fish, liberally suplemented by the national drink, banana cider. After the hands have been washed with a banana stem sponge, these meals are eaten in a little porch, around a space covered with green leaves.

A glance at the Baganda themselves shows us a people belonging to the Bantu race, though differing widely from other negroes in their habits. They are possessed of some fine qualities, and exhibit considerable skill as workers in iron, brass and copper, in dressing skins and in basket making. The field work is left for the women, who often dress with great neatness. Their long robes are fabricated of fig-tree bark or of calico, and ornaments of various sort are worn about the neck, wrists and waist. Soap, made from plantain peelings, is used by the higher classes and their robes are sometimes of snowy whiteness. The women are the barbers, and they, as also the men and children, are shaved entirely about once a month. The higher classes are idle, a trait characteristic to some degree of all.

Socially these people are divided into clans, distinguished by clan animals, which are practically their totems. *Woman* occupies a subordinate position and polygamy prevails. The *peasants* are little better than slaves, being attached to some master, whom, however, they have a right to choose. *Slaves* are possessed by all classes, even the peasants. Their condition can be guessed from the preference of the women of a vanquished tribe who all preferred death to slavery. *Different communities* prey upon each other, soldiers following their chiefs to battle much as in feudal times. Even in neighborhoods where all are supposed to be friends the weak could be openly robbed, with no redress. *Laws* were Draconian, and even the cutting off of hands, feet, ears, nose, or lips was considered a minor punishment. Gross offences against society were avenged by hacking to pieces with sharp strips of reed, or cutting off the limbs, after which the luckless victim was slowly roasted.

Their *religion* included a belief in Katonga, a supreme Creator, but as he was said to have delegated his authority to spirits, *lubares*, they were most highly regarded, especially Mukasa, the Lubare of the lake. Spirits of the earthquake, of thunder, and of various other natural phenomena, as well as of certain persons, were feared, though no worship beyond the erection of roadside shrines and the suspension of charms and amulets on doors or on the person seemed to be given them.

Uganda's Royal Family. A legendary Kintu was the reputed founder of the monarchy, though Captain Speke believes the government to have been established only nine generations ago. The royal family are of Bahuma extraction. *Mtesa*, the first king known to the Europeans, and who received Mackay, was a capricious and sometimes bloodthirsty ruler, deserving his name, which Reclus translates as "he who makes all tremble." The same authority says that he had seven thousand wives; but of these, as of every king's harem, only two possessed regal power. These were the *Namasole* or Queen mother, and the *Lubuga* or Queen-sister, one of the princesses. The king appointed his own chiefs and council and was more or less despotic, as was his prime minister and judge, the Katikiro. On the whole, Mtesa showed himself a man of considerable sympathy and enlightenment, and helped, rather than hindered, the missionaries in their work.

His son, *Mwanga*, the present ruler, succeeded his father in 1884, being then eighteen. He was vain, weak and vicious. Subject to fits of almost demoniacal madness, the missionaries were often in danger of their life, while bloody persecutions were once and again visited on their converts. Mackay was the person who was most necessary to him, though in July, 1887, even he was driven away to the south of the Lake. Though temporarily dethroned at the time of the revolution, he, more than his father, has been a vital factor in the spread of Christianity in Equatorial Africa.

Summary of Mackay's Work in Central Africa. In *1878* Mackay begins missionary buildings. Knowing Suahili, he prints Scripture portions in that tongue. He also reads and explains them to the people, aided by Mtesa and the Katikiro. . . . *1879* witnesses arrival of French Catholic priests, who denounce the missionaries as liars. Embassy sent by Mtesa to England. From June to November great peace, Mtesa ordering chiefs, pages and soldiers to learn the alphabet, and Mackay being on visiting terms with all the chiefs in the capital. In December, Mukasa, representing the Spirit of the Lake, influences Mtesa to return to heathenism. Mackay is so active in his opposition to witchcraft that he is called Anti-Mukasa. . . . *1880* is a year of great trial. Arabs circulate report that Mackay is an insane murderer. Though missionaries are in great danger, they teach lads who come to them. . . . *1881*. New era begins in March, when embassay returned from England. Portions of New Testament, hymns and texts are tentatively translated. . . . *1882*. First five converts of the mission are baptized and the French priests depart. . . . *1883*. Mackay had now printed the Lord's Prayer, Creed, Decalogue, a Text-book of Theology and Selected Texts bearing on duties of subjects and sovereign, as also spelling sheets in Luganda. Two of Mtesa's daughters learners and one is baptized. Twenty-one Christians meet around communion table. Mackay builds the "Eleanor," at south end of lake, doing the work himself. . . . *1884*. Mtesa dies and trouble arises with Mwanga's accession. At close of the year eighty-eight had been baptized in all, and two of Mtesa's daughters and one granddaughter were in the church. The Lubuga, or Queen-sister, a baptized Christian. . . . *1885*. Beginning of persecution, three boy converts being roasted to death. New English missionaries not arriving, Mwanga invites back the French priests. Bishop Hannington murdered in October. Mackay's life, often in danger, is spared on account of his mechanical skill. In November first sheet of Matthew in Luganda printed. . . . *1886*. The year of "The Great Tribulation," the church in exile. In spring bitter persecution breaks out and fifty or sixty Romanist and Protestant converts, who die of fire or the sword, display a fortitude unsurpassed in Apostolic times. Midnight interviews continue, and twenty baptisms take place within a month of the martyrdom. Dr Junker, a Russian traveler, is aided by Mackay to escape from Mwanga. . . . *1887*. Mackay alone in Uganda. In March entire Luganda Matthew corrected in manuscript. Expelled to south of lake and never returns. Gordon takes his place at the capital. . . . *1888*. Year of revolutions, the first one due to Mwanga's attempt to destroy Christian officers. Mwanga exiled and Kiwewa king, with Romanist and Protestant as two chief officers. Temporary religious freedom and prosperity broken by second rebellion—Mohammedan. Missionaries again expelled Uganda. Mackay offers exiled Mwanga protection. . . . *1889.* Romanists advise Mwanga's forcible restoration. Protestants, advised by Mackay not to use force, join Romanists before his reply is received. A third revolution meanwhile ends in Kiwewa's death and Kalema's enthronement. Mwanga, at first unsuccessful, as a penitent suppliant, beseeches Mackay to reinstate him. Christian army vanquishes Kalema and Mwanga is restored as king, with Protestant Kagwa Apollo as prime minister. The king appeals to British East African Company. Mackay revises his Luganda St John, prints, constructs wagon for hauling boat timber, and finally finishes its steam engine and pumps. In August Stanley with Emin and 800 people visits him. . . . *1890.* Mwanga makes treaty with Germans leading to division among Christians. Missionaries advise submission and church prospers until torn with grief by news of Mackay's death which occurred in February. A detailed account of these years is full of interest, but only leading features of the master workman's character and labors can be touched upon.

Some Personal Characteristics. *Social qualities*, so necessary to a pioneer, were quite prominent in Mackay. From the children who instinctively gathered about him, to Lkonge, Smith and O'Neill's murderer, and the two imperious kings of Uganda, there was not one, unless it were the Arabs, who did not yield before his winning friendliness. Mackay's *bravery* was equally marked, and few men have been called upon to so frequently exhibit it. His *resolution* was such that the king involuntarily exclaimed at a signal exhibition of it, "Mackay, you are a *man!*" Marvellous *perseverance* was his and with Carey he could explain much of his success by, "I can plod." Trained during the first two years in the school of *patience*, he exhibited it when his colleagues utterly lost theirs. *Diligence* is absolutely necessary where one lives in an atmosphere of interruptions, and here Mackay is a model for the moment miser. *Foresight*, to which he attributed much of his countrymen's success in engineering, characterized his entire missionary life.

African experiences did not destroy his *intellectuality*.

"Books! Mackay has thousands of books; in the dining room, bedroom, the church, everywhere. Books! ah, loads upon loads of them!" is the ejaculation of a Zanzibar headman, quoted by Stanley. These volumes covered the field of African discovery, the latest scientific utterances, the strongest secular periodicals, the best devotional and theological writings, and current religious and missionary magazines, among which he especially values "The Missionary Review of the World,"—all these enlivened by productions as widely different as "Helen's Babies," and the plays of Shakespere. Africa by its many problems marvellously broadened a mind already admirably trained.

The *hidden life* of Mackay was deep and vital. The *Bible* was the man of his daily counsel, and he speaks of Alford's New Testament as falling to pieces in his hands. An old African letter of his reads: "I feel every day that it is only by prayerful reading of much of God's own Word that I can in any way succeed in living as a Christian. . . . It is just as hard here as in Berlin, or anywhere else, to keep in the right path." Like every missionary, he learned on the field, as never at home, the power of *prayer*. Alone often, and amid dangers that made the bravest quail, he was not alone, for he communed with the Almighty in the secret place, and like William of Orange, was "calm in the midst of storms." His prayer life, linked on to the study and teaching of the Word, begot in him a Paton-like *trust* in God.

A life so dowered, and so reënforced by divine grace, could only be a *consecrated* one. Work he must while it was day; work always and with every one, though most profitably perhaps with evening Nicodemuses, despised Samaritan women and youthful Davids of the court. So consecrated was he to Africa that only a month before his death, when it was proposed that he return to England, he replied, "But what is this you write—'Come home?' Surely now, in our terrible dearth of workers, it is not the time for any one to desert his post."

Mackay's Program. The *eightfold aim* underlying his labors seems to have been: to disarm the prejudice felt by most newly visited tribes, especially in a land where

Arab slavers have terrorized the people; to win their abiding friendship, and, so far as possible, enter into blood-brotherhood with influential chiefs; to destroy the dependent, beggarly spirit entertained toward the missionary; to render noble and manifestly useful manual labor, so despised by influential Africans; to enter perpetual protest against cruel and unjust laws; to do everything possible to drive out Africa's triad of evils, rum, slavery and war; to educate in everything the nation; above all and in all, to win by his teachings and life, souls for Uganda and for God.

The Mechanical Missionary. As an industrial missionary Mackay felt that he could do his work best. It is true that his letters repeatedly speak of the irksomeness of such a ministry, and he even went so far as to attempt to remove a disability existing in the case of laymen, by studying for orders in the Church of England. Yet sober reflection induced him to continue in his less exalted sphere labors which were so signally blest. His grimy hands, whirling lathe and grindstone, marvellous machine which charmed paper so that it talked, the unending application of rotary motion, so largely unknown to the Baganda, were *object lessons* which often elicited clapping of hands and the chorus *Makay lubare! Makay lubare dalai!*—Mackay is the great spirit, he is truly the great spirit!

The *usefulness* of his service commended him to king and subject alike. Repaired guns, healed bodies,—for Mackay was perforce a lay physician,—the wonderful cart upon which he could with one hand move a tree that 200 men had wasted their strength upon, the well on a side-hill spitting out through a battered pump pure water, bridges and roads, monster flagstaff for the king, the two royal coffins, especialy the Namasole's, as large as a cottage and requiring many workmen and a month of Mackay's best strength,—these and a host of other miracles wrought by the canny Highlander, made him indispensable. He was not only always busy, but he so often spoke to the people of the nobility of work, its utility and necessity, that they called him *Mzungu-wa Kazi*, white man of work. "His readiness of resource in emergency (for which his training as an engineer had peculiarly fitted him)," was most useful to the

Mission also; for because of it starvation was repeatedly held at bay, and in times of hostility, even life was spared. His labors as an industrial missionary justified—at least for uncivilized lands—*his thesis:* "Mechanical work is probably as legitimate an aid to missions as medical; nor do I see why one should not be as helpful to missionary work as the other, except for the difficulty of getting out of the rut our ideas run in." Lovedale in South Africa conspicuously emphasizes Mackay's view.

Among the People. Their presence in Mackay's house or shop, by night and by day, left little time for visits among them; but when such opportunities offered he gladly embraced them. Eating with them in their tiny porches, journeying with friend and foe, gave him glimpses into their speech and life and thought, which were denied him when his foreign environment made them the questioners and learners. If his companions were Christians, he was in a third heaven of bliss. Their upbuilding and his joy in the converts reminds one of Paul's experiences. Nor could he hold his peace when heathenism was rampant, as when the fleet of fourteen canoes in which he sailed robbed three Buzongora canoes. His protest and threat to spear the captain of the fleet unless the property was restored, caused robbers and robbed to be stronger friends than before. This was the same fleet whose belief in potent charms was shattered by the missionary who bought one, discoursed on its weakness and on God's power and then proved his words by burning it in a fire lighted by a small pocket lens,— a good illustration of his method of teaching and preaching.

At Court. Naturally such a man was frequently called to stand before kings; though much to his relief, his colleagues, especially the witty O'Flaherty, relieved him of much of this labor. Of course he was *a priest of civilization* there. At one time bringing in and explaining a glazier's diamond and an ox yoke, Mtesa says, "There must remain nothing more for white men to know—they know everything." At another, Mackay writes out a list of sanitary regulations intended to prevent and stay the terrible ravages of the plague, and Uganda suddenly begins to clean house. In general he embraces every proper opportunity to amplify a text which greatly impressed the king, "My forefathers made the WIND their slave; then they put WATER in the chain; next they enslaved STEAM; but now the terrible LIGHTNING is the white man's slave, and a a capital one it is too!"

But destructive work needed to be done before the kingdom was free to enter upon the higher civilization. *Superstitions*, especially those connected with the Neptune of the lake, the great Mukasa, bound king and peasant with steel fetters. Mackay boldly takes his stand on the Scriptures, and as a "Servant of Almighty God," begs the king to have nothing to do with the lubare. In Socratic style he makes all admit that if he is a god, there are two gods in Uganda, the Almighty and Mukasa; if he is a man,—the one in question was a woman, he afterwards learned,—there are two kings in the land, Mtesa, whom all honor, and Mukasa, who pretends to be supreme, and who practically incites to rebellion. Though the witch had her way with the king, the people could say nothing in answer to such logic.

Hardly less obstructive to Africa's civilization is *slavery* and the Scotchman goes boldly before the greatest slave hunter of his day where, with Huxley's plates to illustrate the circulation of the blood, "he dwelt on the perfection of the human body, which no man can make, nor all the men in the world; and yet the Arabs wished to buy a human being with an immortal soul, for a bit of soap!" The interested king, can only add as a corollary to this demonstration, "From henceforth no slave shall be sold out of the country."

As a *preacher of righteousness* Mackay is a second Paul before Agrippa. Diplomatic, fearless of death, constantly appealing to "the Book," he illustrates and enforces the truth of God, whether it bears on subjects persecuted for righteousness' sake, religious liberty for all faiths, or kings' vices and their need of a Saviour. Adversaries were at court, especially the Arabs, who regarded the missionary as their worst foe because opposed to slavery. Mackay is again a Paul answering Islam's Tertullus, and righteousness and truth are vindicated. Alas that such preaching found in Mtesa and Mwanga an Agrippa and a Felix!

The Wider Court. Mackay's voice was heard in Christian Europe. Africa's open sores and her "heart disease," needed foreign physicians. Chapters XII., XIV.-XVI. of " Mackay of Uganda," are wise utterances of a missionary statesman, and they were heeded. Already the measures pleaded for have been partially adopted, namely, limitation in sales of arms, ammunition and rum, increased vigilance along the coast, a cordon of police in the interior, and improved communications with Central Africa. The railroad to the Lake, 657 miles long, has already reached Dunantabe, and cheapened transportation—which formerly cost $1400 a ton and countless lives—will soon change Uganda.

Mackay has been charged with *interfering with African politics*, but this interference was in the interests of outraged humanity and international justice. Tempting offers to become an officer under General Gordon and the Imperial East African Company were not accepted, because he was not so much a British citizen as an embassador of the Prince of Peace appointed to Central Africa to establish there the Kingdom of Heaven. To this cause he summons Christendom's best blood in his last message.

Mackay's Passing. A real king of Uganda, Carlyle's canny man, had done his work. The excalibar, wrought by his mechanical genius, was to disappear from the mighty Lake. Chiefs and commoners—become members of his Table Round, the Church Council—had caught his spirit. On February 8th, 1890, the summons came to the exile at Usambiro. Fever, Africa's executioner, silenced the craftsman and the expositor of John's Gospel, and after four days of delirium, in which solicitude for converts, plans for future work, and longings for fresh laborers found expression, the soul of St Paul of Uganda, flitted upward to the dear home land.

"All hail the power of Jesus' name" was sung by Baganda boys over his open grave, and then they went back to establish the 200 churches of to-day, to build a cathedral accommodating 7000, and to invite the multitudes who are now pressing into the Kingdom. Hannington wrote from the northeast of the lake : "Mackay's name seems quite a household word; I constantly hear it, but of the others I scarce ever hear a word." Similarly, Jephson, one of Stanley's officers, writing of the southwestern lake region, says: "For many days before we reached his Mission, we heard from the natives of Mackay, nothing but Mackay—they seemed to care for and know no one else. Such a man cannot die in Africa; and in Britain, when in May of 1895, the first detachment of ladies to enter Uganda and five new men were sent to reap in the fields where Mackay had sown, his old letters were the clarion note which sounded the charge. "He being dead yet speaketh."

SUGGESTED READINGS.

Ashe: Chronicles of Uganda, (1894), Pp. 55-143.
Two Kings of Uganda, (1889), Ch. XXIII.
Church Misssionary Gleaner, May, 1896.
Church Missionary Intelligencer, April and May, 1896.
Drummond: Tropical Africa, (1888), Ch. IV.
Encyclopædia of Missions, (1891), Articles Church Missionary Society and Alexander M. Mackay.
Harrison: Story of the Life of Mackay of Uganda, (1891), Chs. VI-XXI,
Larned: History for Ready Reference, (1895), Vol. V., Article Uganda.
Latimer: Europe in Africa in the Nineteenth Century, (1895), Ch. VII.
Lugard: Rise of Our East African Empire, (1893), Vol I., Chs. VII., VIII.
Peters: New light on Dark Africa, (1890), Pp. 379, ff.
Reclus: Universal Geography, Vol. X., Pp. 88, ff.
Stanley: In Darkest Africa, (1890), Vol, II., Pp, 423-431.
White: The Development of Africa, (1890), Chs. V., VI., IX.
Wilson and Felkin: Uganda, (1882), Vol. I., V., VII., VIII.
Harrison: Mackay of Uganda, (1890), Description of the People, V., VII.; Tide ebbs and flows, Chs. VIII.; Tribulation, Chs. IX-XI.; African Problems, Chs. XII., XIV-XVI.; Last Things, Chs. XIII., XVII.

www.ingramcontent.com/pod-product-compliance
Lightning Source LLC
Chambersburg PA
CBHW020144170426
43199CB00010B/882